11/6 ᒐ 11/8×ᒐ

W9-AHA-679

Lifeline
BIOGRAPHIES

WILL SMITH
Box Office Superstar

by Matt Doeden

Twenty-First Century Books · Minneapolis

Twenty-First Century Books
A division of Lerner Publishing Group, Inc.
241 First Avenue North
Minneapolis, MN 55401 U.S.A.

Website address: www.lernerbooks.com

Library of Congress Cataloging-in-Publication Data

Doeden, Matt.
    Will Smith : box office superstar / by Matt Doeden.
        p.   cm. — (USA today lifeline biographies)
    Includes bibliographical references and index.
    Includes filmography and discography.
    ISBN 978–0–7613–4265–6 (lib. bdg. : alk. paper)
    1. Smith, Will, 1968-—Juvenile literature. 2. Actors—United States—Biography—
Juvenile literature. 3. Rap musicians—United States—Biography—Juvenile literature.
I. Title.
PN2287.S612D64 2010
791.4302'8092—dc22 [B]   2008053300

Manufactured in the United States of America
1 2 3 4 5 6 – PA – 15 14 13 12 11 10

USA TODAY Lifeline BIOGRAPHIES

On the set: Will goofs around on the set of *The Fresh Prince of Bel-Air* in 1990.

Jump Start

In 1990 a meeting on a California talk show changed Will Smith's life. If the meeting hadn't happened, the actor and rapper might never have gained his great success.

Will had already made—and spent—a fortune as the rapper known as the Fresh Prince. He was deeply in debt. He owed more money in taxes than he had in his bank accounts. His music career was stalling. Will had come to California in hopes of starting an acting career. There was just one problem. He had never really acted before.

Then, in 1989, Will met Benny Medina. They were at a taping of *The Arsenio Hall Show*. Medina had led an unusual life. He'd spent his childhood in Watts, a poor neighborhood in Los Angeles. His mother had died, and his father had left him. He'd been sent from one foster home to the next. He finally ended up living with a rich family. Eventually, Medina got into the music business. By the time he met Will, Medina was a producer for Warner Bros. Records. He wanted to make a TV show based on his life. He thought Will would be perfect for the lead role.

From that meeting, everything moved quickly. Within a month, the NBC television network had agreed to do the show. Will would be the

Star power: Will's personality helped land him the lead role on a new television series in 1990.

May 29, 1990

NBC is giving 'Fresh Prince' the royal treatment

<u>From the Pages of USA TODAY</u> The premise is simple: A sassy black kid from the ghetto moves in with a straight-laced, upper-class black family in a ritzy Los Angeles neighborhood. Both have different ways of life, but they come to respect each other.

The Fresh Prince of Bel-Air is the old fish out of water scenario, with shades of *Diff'rent Strokes*, and NBC is touting it as a Cosby-sized hit. The new fall sitcom stars rapper Will Smith of D.J. Jazzy Jeff & the Fresh Prince. NBC Entertainment president Brandon Tartikoff is predicting it will be NBC's first "hit-the-ground running hit" since *The Golden Girls* in 1985. He says *Prince* was NBC's highest-testing comedy pilot ever, better even than Cosby, and Smith is going to be "a big, breakout star."

Tartikoff brought Smith to New York and Chicago last week to meet advertisers, comparing Smith's comedy talents to those of another former NBC star, Eddie Murphy. "That stuff made me nervous," said Smith, 21, from Philadelphia, where he was in the studio over the weekend recording a new album with D.J. Jazzy Jeff. "There's no way I could be compared with Eddie. He's the ultimate."

— Jefferson Graham

star. Borrowing from Will's rapping nickname, producers named the show *The Fresh Prince of Bel-Air*. (Bel-Air is a wealthy neighborhood in Los Angeles.) They put a cast of professional actors around Will and began taping. The show first aired in September 1990. It got great ratings. Will's life would never be the same.

USA TODAY

CHAPTER ONE

Hometown: Will was born in West Philadelphia, Pennsylvania, in 1968. Almost two million people lived in Philadelphia *(above)* at that time. It was the fourth-largest city in the United States.

Young Will

Willard C. Smith Jr. was born September 25, 1968, in West Philadelphia, Pennsylvania. He was the second child of Caroline and Willard Smith Sr.

Will's family life was good. His dad owned a refrigeration business called Arcac. Caroline worked for the local board of education. Will had an older sister, Pamela. Later, the family grew with a younger brother, Harry, and sister, Ellen. The family lived in a middle-class neighborhood called Wynnefield. Like most people in Wynnefield, the Smiths weren't rich. But they had enough money to live on.

> Will's younger brother, Harry, grew up to be Will's accountant and business partner.

From an early age, Will wanted to be heard. His mother says he learned to talk before he learned to walk. He loved books. His favorites were by Dr. Seuss. His parents read him Seuss's rhymes almost every night. Years later, Will wondered whether the rhymes might have inspired him to rap. "If you listen to them in a certain way," he said, "[Dr. Seuss] books . . . sound a lot like hip-hop [music]."

As a former member of the U.S. Air Force, Willard Sr. was strict. He expected his children to behave. He wasn't afraid to punish them. Will's mouth often got him in trouble. "It was a real military kind of house," Will remembered. "There was a military type of structure and discipline."

But there was also plenty of love in the house. "There's a certain level of confidence and self-esteem that comes from knowing . . . that someone loves you," he said of his childhood. "It's not based on whether my homework's done. Just because I'm me, these people love me. So it's like, I know I'm good. How can I let the world know?"

The Center of Attention

Even with Willard's rules, the Smith family was fun loving. Everyone had a good sense of humor. The family liked to joke with one another. More than anyone, Will wanted to be the center of attention. Whether it was at school or at the dinner table, Will enjoyed being noticed.

Will's grandmother Helen Bright saw that Will craved the spotlight. She often set up plays for her church. She made sure Will always had a part. As expected, her grandson loved having all eyes on him.

Work Ethic

Willard Sr. wanted his children to share his work ethic. When Will was fifteen, his dad gave him and Harry a summer project. They had to tear down—and rebuild—a brick wall at the Smith home. At first, the boys complained. They said that the job was too big. They could never get it done. But Willard insisted that they could—and would—do it.

So the boys got to work. They mixed cement and laid bricks. Slowly, they built a new wall. The project took most of the summer. But they finished it. It was a lesson that Willard wanted his sons to remember. As the boys stood admiring their work, Willard told them they could never again say there was something they couldn't do.

Life lesson: Will's father taught his sons through action—he had them build a brick wall by themselves.

IN FOCUS

"Rapper's Delight"

In 1979 a group called the Sugar Hill Gang released the song "Rapper's Delight." It made people aware of rap music. "Rapper's Delight" is an amazing fifteen minutes long. But that didn't stop it from being played a lot on the radio.

"Rapper's Delight" was the first rap song that Will and many other future rappers heard. But the song doesn't talk about any of the political or urban issues that have since become important in rap. Modern rap fans might laugh at the song, but it played a big part in bringing rap to the mainstream.

Sugar Hill Gang: "Rapper's Delight" helped bring rap and hip-hop music into the mainstream and made *(from left)* Big Bank Hank, Wonder Mike, and Master Gee famous.

Education was important to Will's mother. Caroline didn't think public school was good enough for her children. So Will spent kindergarten through eighth grade at a private school called Our Lady of Lourdes. He developed many interests there. He liked English and poetry. Dinosaurs and science fascinated him. He also loved music, sports, and goofing around with his friends. Even at a young age, Will was the class clown. He always had a joke to share.

"It's always been fun for me to tell a story and make people laugh," he explained. "I've always been a show-off, and uncomfortable when people weren't looking at me."

Caroline saw that Will had a talent for music. She encouraged him and his brothers and sisters to take up the arts. She wanted Will to learn to play several instruments. The family even formed their own jazz group. They played for themselves at home. Will's instrument was the drums. He loved music with a strong beat.

In 1980, when Will was twelve years old, he heard a song called "Rapper's Delight" on the radio. He'd just discovered a new kind of music: rap. The rhythms of rap seemed to be made for Will. Before long, he was dreaming up raps of his own. Caroline encouraged him. But she never thought anything would come of his hobby.

Paying attention: This photo of Will appeared in his senior high school yearbook. Will is in his science class.

Prince Charming

■ ■ ■ ■

Our Lady of Lourdes stopped at the eighth grade. So in 1982, Will moved on to Overbrook High. Overbrook was a public school. It was a big change for Will. For most of his school years, Will had been mostly with white children. At Overbrook he had to fit in with more African American students. Will's outgoing personality helped him make friends at his new school.

"I went to school with all white people for nine years and then all black people for three years," he said. "That helped me, because I have a great understanding of what black people think is funny and what white people think is funny. I'm able to find a joke that everyone thinks is [funny], the record everyone thinks is moving, or a great dance record."

> Will was a tall, skinny kid. By the age of thirteen, he already stood at his adult height—6 feet 2 inches (2 meters).

Will's personality wasn't just a hit with his fellow students. His teachers also noticed his charm. Will wasn't a fan of doing homework. But he learned to sweet-talk his way out of trouble. The teachers began calling him Prince Charming for the way he used charm to get by.

Young Rapper

Will's love for rap was growing. He was always coming up with new rhymes. He sang them at school and at home. Caroline enjoyed her son's passion. But rap wasn't her sort of music. She thought it was a fad.

Will didn't see it that way. He dreamed about a career in rap. But he wasn't just thinking about being a rapper. He also dreamed about being a DJ (disc jockey). In rap

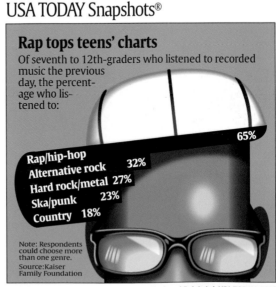

USA TODAY Snapshots®

Rap tops teens' charts
Of seventh to 12th-graders who listened to recorded music the previous day, the percentage who listened to:

65%

Rap/hip-hop
Alternative rock 32%
Hard rock/metal 27%
Ska/punk 23%
Country 18%

Note: Respondents could choose more than one genre.
Source: Kaiser Family Foundation

By Rebecca Pollack and Bob Laird, USA TODAY, 2005

music, the DJ has a key role. The DJ uses a turntable (record player) and record albums to create new sounds that go along with the raps.

Will followed his dream. He served as a DJ for friends. Meanwhile, rap was getting bigger and bigger. But some people found rap threatening. They linked it to rough lifestyles and drug use. Willard Sr. was worried about the track his son was on. So he drove Will into one of Philadelphia's toughest neighborhoods. There, he pointed at people living on the streets. "That is what people look like when they're on drugs," he told his son.

Will's parents divorced in 1981. The children lived with Caroline but saw Will Sr. often.

The lesson stuck. Will says he never had any interest in drugs. But his father's feelings didn't stop his love of rap. In 1982, by the age of fourteen, he had formed a rap duo with his friend Clarence Holmes. Clarence went by the name Ready Rock-C. Will took on the name

Performing partners: Will *(center)* performed with both Ready Rock-C *(left)* and DJ Jazzy Jeff *(right)* in the 1980s.

Fresh Prince. The name was a play on the nickname his teachers had given him. Together, the Fresh Prince and Ready Rock-C contacted a record label. They wanted to make an album. Record producer Dana Goodman turned them down. But he also told them to keep working and try again.

A New Partner

Will kept at it. He played at parties. He even earned a few dollars along the way. In the summer of 1985, when Will was sixteen, he met Jeff Townes. Jeff was a DJ who went by the name DJ Jazzy Jeff. He earned his nickname because he used jazz records on his turntable. He had a small but loyal fan base in Philadelphia. Will went to a party to see him play.

Will enjoyed Jeff's music. He asked the DJ if he could join him on-stage for a rap. Jeff agreed. The two hit it off right away. "He started rapping and I started cutting [making sounds on the turntable], and it was like natural chemistry," Jeff said. "He flowed with what I did

IN FOCUS

Jazzy Jeff

Jeff Townes was born January 22, 1965, in Philadelphia. Like Will, he'd been hooked from the moment he first heard rap. He was fascinated by DJs and how they used records to create new sounds. By the age of ten, he had his own DJ setup. Soon he was performing for friends, for family, and at small parties. Most DJs focused on hip-hop and soul classics. Jeff's love for jazz set him apart. An appearance at a local radio station made a name for the young DJ. Soon he was playing all over Philadelphia. He met Will at one of these performances.

and I flowed exactly with what he did and we both knew it. We just clicked the whole night long." The musicians complemented each other perfectly.

Jeff was four years older than Will. He had more experience. But he couldn't get the young rapper out of his mind. He even dreamed of Will that night. The next day, Jeff had made up his mind. He had to get Will's phone number so they could form a duo. He knew that DJ Jazzy Jeff and the Fresh Prince could be a hit. Will was eager to team up with his new friend.

Will and Jeff began working on raps. Despite their age difference, they got along well. They had the same taste in music. They had similar senses of humor. And they shared a passion for what they were

Dynamic duo: Will and DJ Jazzy Jeff *(left)* posed for this picture in the 1980s.

doing. Together, they were making music that was better than anything either had done alone.

At the end of the summer, the duo met with Goodman about recording a single. A single is one song, rather than a full-length album. This time, Goodman agreed to give them a shot. DJ Jazzy Jeff and the Fresh Prince were set to record their song "Girls Ain't Nothing but Trouble" for the Word-Up record label.

If Will would have had his way, his life might have become just about music. But his mother wouldn't let that happen. That fall Will started his senior year of high school. She insisted that his studies come first. Will's intelligence was clear to his teachers. They wanted him to get ready for college, not for a rap career.

Will honored his mom's wishes and focused on school. He still loved science. And he did well on his college entrance exams. Caroline knew that her son could get into a good college, so she encouraged him to apply. After all, she thought, going to college would help ensure her son's future. His rapping couldn't do that.

Radio Waves

Will had a different point of view. In 1986, during his senior year at Overbrook, "Girls Ain't Nothing but Trouble" was released. The song is about a boy and all of his girl troubles. It first was played on Philadelphia radio stations. But then the song's popularity grew. A record label called Jive Records offered Will and Jeff thirty thousand dollars for the rights to the song. They agreed. Soon the song was playing on radio stations across the country. In no time, the single had sold one hundred thousand copies.

DJ Jazzy Jeff and the Fresh Prince had a sound that was different from mainstream rap. At the time, most rap was serious. Rappers rhymed about crime and racism. By contrast, Will's rhymes were pure fun. It was a form of rap that many teens adored—and their parents didn't hate. As Will's nickname suggested, it was fresh and new.

Still, the song had its critics. Hard-core rap fans rejected it. They said that two middle-class boys couldn't write real rap. Others

claimed that the song in-
sulted women. Will dis-
agreed. "That's a ridicu-
lous . . . opinion," he said.
"The rap is a personal
story, told with a sense
of humor."

The sudden success left
Will with a hard decision.
Caroline badly wanted her
son to go to college. Will
knew that going to college
was a big opportunity.
But on the other hand,
Will was a high school senior with a hit song. Kids
around the country knew
who he was. He could
hear himself on the radio
and see himself on MTV.

High school: Will was well liked by his fellow
students and the teachers at his high school.
This photo was taken during his senior year.

Rap was his passion. And it finally looked like a real career choice.

After a lot of thought, Will made up his mind. He had to follow his
heart. He had dreamed of being a rapper. That chance might never
come again. So in 1986—while still in high school—Will joined Jeff in
the studio to record their first full-length album, *Rock the House*. Will's
old music partner, Ready Rock-C, joined them.

Rock the House came out in 1987. It was a success. The album shot
up the music charts. It soon went gold (sold five hundred thousand
copies). The money was coming in fast. Even Will's parents had a hard
time questioning his choice. Willard Sr. told his son that he should give
music a year. If it didn't work out, he could go to college then.

Despite his popularity, Will hardly led the life of a star. He still lived
at home. DJ Jazzy Jeff and the Fresh Prince didn't even go on tour to

support their album. Instead, they wanted to put out another album right away, while they were still hot. They knew that an act could be popular one day and forgotten the next. They weren't about to let people forget them.

The DJ and the Rapper

Will and Jeff didn't want just another album. They dreamed of creating something unique. They hoped to make music that kids would love with lyrics their parents would be proud of. They started writing. The rhymes began flowing. They had so much good material that choosing which songs to put on their album was a challenge.

Their solution was simple. The album, titled *He's the DJ, I'm the Rapper*, would be a double album. The idea of putting out a double

Hard at work: The rap duo worked on their albums and promoted their style in the 1980s.

album wasn't unusual in the world of rock and roll. But for rap, it was groundbreaking. With seventeen songs, *He's the DJ, I'm the Rapper* was finally released in 1988.

The album's sound was true to what Will and Jeff had started two years before. The rhymes were crisp and clean. Will sang about common teenage concerns. The album had lots of humor. It lacked the strong language common to many rap albums of the time. Will's writing skills were more polished. Jeff's backgrounds were richer. It was just the radio-friendly kind of release that the duo's fans had been hoping for.

The single that drove album sales was the lighthearted "Parents Just Don't Understand." The song is written from the viewpoint of a teen who is clothes shopping with his mother. It was a huge hit. The video showed Will living out the story. It was among the most popular on MTV. "Parents Just Don't Understand" did better than "Girls Ain't Nothing but Trouble." To the surprise of many, DJ Jazzy Jeff and the Fresh Prince weren't just a one-hit wonder.

Criticism and Praise

Many teens—and their parents—were grateful for Will's family-friendly lyrics. But his style again drew criticism from the rap world. Some rappers continued to insist that Will's upbeat lyrics weren't really rap. A rapper called Big Daddy Kane even said that Will wasn't writing for African Americans. He was appealing to white fans, Kane said. Will was betraying rap's African American roots.

"I don't think anybody can [say] what's black and what's not black," Will said in an interview. "Big Daddy Kane . . . doesn't realize what black really means. . . . We're trying to show the world, and black kids, that you can dress nicely and speak well and still be considered black. Our music is black music."

Unlike many rap acts of the time, Will and Jeff hadn't grown up in poverty. Their lives hadn't been filled with gangs and violence. And they refused to apologize for that. Their album sales proved that

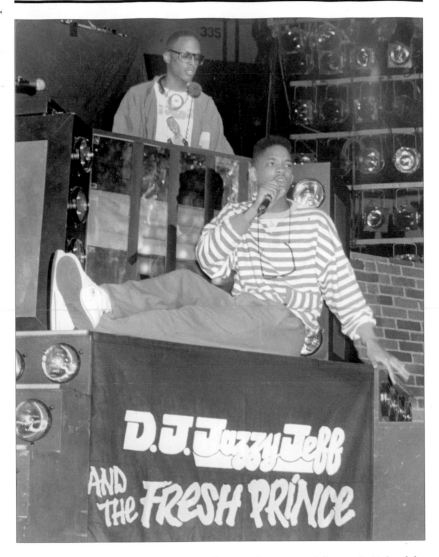

On the road: Will and DJ Jazzy Jeff perform at the Nassau Coliseum in Uniondale, New York, in 1988.

their talent was what mattered, not their backgrounds. Within a few months, *He's the DJ, I'm the Rapper* had sold more than three million copies. Fans of all races were enjoying their music. In spite of the criticism, the album was a success.

This time around, Will and Jeff took their show on the road. They toured with rap legends Run-DMC. While their sounds and lyrics were different, the acts had a lot in common. Run-DMC was another "crossover" act. They had appeal with both white and black fans. Will and Jeff also used humor in their shows. Touring was a new

IN FOCUS

Run-DMC

Run-DMC was one of the biggest rap acts of the 1980s. The group's members included (*below left to right*) Jason "Jam Master Jay" Mizell, Darryl "D.M.C." McDaniels, and Joseph "Run" Simmons. Run-DMC helped bring rap into the mainstream. They were the first rap group to air a video on MTV. Their album *Run-DMC* was the first rap album to go gold.

Run-DMC's most famous song is a hip-hop version of a rock song—Aerosmith's "Walk This Way." The song includes vocals from Aerosmith lead singer Steven Tyler. It was a huge crossover hit.

experience for Will and Jeff. They reached their fans in a way they never had before.

"We like to give the audience a lesson in rap," Jeff said of their shows. "It's not hard, anyone can do it. It's not about black or white, it's just about having fun."

As 1989 began, DJ Jazzy Jeff and the Fresh Prince found even more success. In January they won two American Music Awards for Favorite Rap Album and Favorite Rap Artists. Next, "Parents Just Don't Understand" received a Grammy nomination for the new category, Best Rap Performance. A Grammy is the music industry's highest honor. The young men were excited when they learned of the nomination. But then they found out that the Best Rap Performance award would not be given out with the main televised awards. Instead, it would be included in a separate group of awards that show organizers didn't think were big enough for TV.

Two for two: DJ Jazzy Jeff and the Fresh Prince took home two American Music Awards in 1989. The duo won Favorite Rap Artist and Favorite Rap Album.

October 16, 1989

Rap duo delivers with punch

From the Pages of
USA TODAY

The USA's most lovable, most awarded rappers have grown up. Or so they claim.

D.J. Jazzy Jeff and the Fresh Prince, whose lightweight, comical "Parents Just Don't Understand" nabbed the first rap Grammy and MTV's first rap video award, are pushing past musical puberty with their third LP, *And in This Corner...* (Jive), out Oct. 31.

Its first single, "I Think I Can Beat Mike Tyson," is just out, boasting the humorous storytelling that sold 2.5 million copies of their last LP, *He's the D.J., I'm the Rapper*, which also nabbed the American Music Awards' first rap honors. That LP addressed polyester shirts, stealing their parents' car and *A Nightmare on Elm Street*'s Freddy Krueger. *This Corner* tackles serious issues. That is, as serious as two middle-class, self-proclaimed nice guys from Philadelphia can be. Issues range from having their own car stolen (Who Stole My Car?) to gold-digging girlfriends (You Got It).

Despite their new-found maturity, the pair is far from the trendy, socially conscious messages of other rappers. "We chose not to preach," says the Prince, who writes the lyrics. "When you preach, children have a tendency not to listen."

The Prince, a poet since high school, has been rapping since he was 13; Jeff began mixing and scratching in his basement at 10. In 1986, the two met at a party. "I got a click when I worked with Prince that I never got with anybody else," says Jeff.

—James T. Jones IV

Will and Jeff felt that this placement was an insult to rap. They protested by not attending the awards. It was their way of making a statement. Still, "Parents Just Don't Understand" won the Grammy. Their absence helped ensure that in future years, rap would have a place on the main stage. They got little credit from mainstream rappers for their protest.

Free Spender

Sales of *He's the DJ, I'm the Rapper* soared. Money was pouring in. Will was turning into a big spender. He hadn't ever known poverty. But the Smiths hadn't been rich either. The money was a huge temptation. Will bought cars and jewelry. He even bought a house with a hot tub, an indoor basketball court, and a pool room. His brother, Harry, moved into the house with him. Will had little self-control. He was spending and spending. He never thought about whether the money would stop coming in.

Willard Sr. warned his son about his spending habits. "What do you need six cars for when you only have one butt?" he asked. But the warning didn't get through. Will kept spending. He threw parties, traveled, and bought gifts for friends and family. One time, he even flew to London and Tokyo just to shop for clothes. After all, Will thought, he had money. Why not spend it? "I went through [money] so fast it made my head spin," Will later said. "I had a problem. Whenever I got a little bored, I'd go shopping."

New experiences: Will's sudden wealth became a huge temptation in the late 1980s. He spent all of his newly made money on cars, gifts, and a house.

Even the recording of his next album was over the top. Will and Jeff rented a house in the Bahamas (islands near Florida). They flew their friends there for a nonstop party. It wasn't a good place to work. The pair finished just four songs.

Will was digging himself into a hole. He managed his own money. He had no help from an accountant. Will thought taxes were coming out of his checks. But he was wrong. He found out he owed millions of dollars to the Internal Revenue Service (IRS). With all of his spending, he didn't have enough money to pay his taxes.

The IRS froze (took over) Will's money and property. By the middle of 1989, he was broke. His big-spending lifestyle ended. "There's nothing more sobering than having six cars and a mansion one day, and you can't even buy gas for the cars the next," Will said. "It hurt, and mentally it was tough . . . but inside, it didn't change. I still had my family, and I could still have a good time. I could still laugh."

Backed into a Corner

Yet the bad news kept coming. Will was counting on his next album, *And in This Corner. . .*, to pay his debts. The album came out at the end of 1989.

The music scene had changed since the release of *He's the DJ, I'm the Rapper*. At that time, Will and Jeff had carved out their own place in the world of hip-hop. But by the time *And in This Corner. . .* came out, the duo had more competition for listeners. And their new album lacked the catchy sounds that had made earlier albums such hits. The album's biggest single, "I Think I Can Beat Mike Tyson," didn't have the wide appeal of their earlier hits.

And in This Corner. . . was by no means a failure. The album sold more than one million copies. But it fell short of what Will had expected. The money it made wasn't enough to get Will out of debt. Worse still, it was clear that Will and Jeff had peaked in popularity with *He's the DJ, I'm the Rapper*.

Will knew he might never reach that level of popularity again. He wasn't ready to leave music behind. But he thought it was time to start following another dream—acting. From his music videos, Will knew he liked being in front of a camera. He was well spoken and good looking. He seemed a natural fit as an actor. So he moved to California. Jeff stayed in Philadelphia. But the pair promised that they'd keep working together.

Shortly after the move, Will met Benny Medina. Within months, Will had gotten the lead role in *The Fresh Prince of Bel-Air*. It was a big career change. Will was determined to make it work. He had to make it work, or he might spend the rest of his life in debt.

Learning to act: Will poses on the set of *The Fresh Prince of Bel-Air* in 1990.

A New Direction

■ ■ ■ ■ ■

The Fresh Prince of Bel-Air took over a key spot in NBC's schedule. It replaced the popular comedy *ALF* on the network's Monday-night lineup. The new show was a family-friendly sitcom. It was about a young man (Smith) whose mother had sent him away from the rough streets of Philadelphia. He went to live with his rich aunt and uncle in Bel-Air, California.

Smith was a great fit for the part. But some people at NBC were unsure about him. After all, he'd never acted. They thought an

USA TODAY

Life

SECTION D

August 24, 1990

Will Smith hip-hops into prime time

From the Pages of
USA TODAY

Will Smith has been assigned a simple task: Deliver NBC its first runaway comedy hit since *The Golden Girls*.

Will who? Rapper Will Smith, the lanky 21-year-old known in the world of hip-hop as the Fresh Prince. The guy who paired with D.J. Jazzy Jeff for the rap anthem, "Parents Just Don't Understand." Can he do it?

"The great black hope," smiles the Prince, trying to remain cool. He has been an actor three days, the time it took to shoot the first episode. Smith wouldn't mind dousing some of the hyperbole swirling around Fresh Prince. Maybe bring the tub-thumping—and the expectations—down a decibel or two. This comparison to [Eddie] Murphy, who exploded into stardom as a young guy via *Saturday Night Live*, is starting to scare him.

"Hey, man, I'm worried about Eddie Murphy walking up to me in a club and challenging me to a joke-off. With God's blessing, I hope to one day be like Eddie Murphy. But it's not today." Others aren't so sure. Smith is so instantly appealing he could charm himself into the hearts of TV viewers and his lack of comedy training won't matter at all.

—Tom Green

experienced actor might be a better choice. But Medina and fellow producer Quincy Jones stood firm. They believed in Smith. They also knew his fame would bring in viewers. They told NBC to give Smith an audition, or test performance.

Smith's audition pleased the NBC executives. "It was clear to me that this guy was a natural," said one of them. "[Smith] read from the script and just nailed it. I sat there thinking, 'Whoa! Just bottle this guy.'"

NBC was eager to cash in on Smith's rapping background. The network had him do a rap for the show's opening theme song. Smith's rhymes perfectly fit the fun nature of the show.

Others worried that Smith's music background could be a drawback. Despite his ease in front of the camera, Smith just wasn't an actor yet. So NBC surrounded him with a talented cast. The experienced

TV family: Will's on-screen family included many experienced actors. The cast was *(clockwise from left)* Karyn Parsons, Joseph Marcell, Janet Hubert, James Avery, Alfonso Ribeiro, Will, and Tatyana M. Ali.

James Avery played Smith's gruff uncle. Sitcom veteran Alfonso Ribeiro took the role of his uptight cousin. Even the cast's youngest member, Tatyana M. Ali, had been acting for six years.

Working with such a good cast made Smith nervous. "I was trying so hard," he said. "I would memorize the entire script. Then I'd be lipping everybody's lines while they were talking."

Critics weren't the only ones who had bad things to say about Smith's acting. Tatyana M. Ali, who played Smith's youngest cousin on the show, was very hard on him. She said she couldn't believe her costar was such a bad actor. But over time, the actors became friends. Smith thought of Tatyana almost as a little sister.

Beginner's mistakes were to be expected. The show's producers were patient. They focused on Smith's strengths—his humor and charm—rather than on areas that needed work. With a lot of effort, the cast finished the pilot (first) episode. NBC tested the pilot with audiences. They loved it. NBC ordered a full season of episodes. The order was a big vote of confidence for a new show.

Hitting the Airwaves

The first show aired on September 10, 1990. The ratings were great. Viewers seemed willing to look past Smith's shortcomings as an actor. His charm seemed to be enough.

"It's a whole different thing being an actor," Smith said. "A rapper is about being completely true to yourself. Being an actor is about changing who you are. You make yourself a different person. You become a different person."

Fans accepted Smith. But many critics did not. They pointed out that his lines lacked emotion. They said that he often spoke too softly. His movements were stiff. He didn't look natural. But slowly, Smith improved. He talked to experienced actors and comedians, such as Bill Cosby and Eddie Murphy. He asked them for advice. He dedicated himself to his new job. He also kept working hard on his music.

IN F⊕CUS

Eddie Murphy

Eddie Murphy, born in 1961 in New York, joined the cast of the popular TV show *Saturday Night Live* in 1980, at the age of nineteen. His quick wit and funny voice made him one of the show favorites. In 1982 Murphy moved to the big screen with the hit movie *48 Hrs.* Two years later, he had another success with *Beverly Hills Cop.* In the years since, Murphy has done dozens more movies, stand-up comedy, and even had a brief singing career.

Big winner: In 2007 Eddie Murphy won a Golden Globe for his performance in *Dreamgirls.*

As expected, Smith got a lot of criticism from the world of rap. Some called him a sellout. Others mocked the family-friendly nature of the show. Again, people accused him of creating entertainment for whites rather than for African Americans. But the criticism was no worse than what Smith was used to. He didn't let it bother him.

When the cast of the show went on break, Smith took steps toward a movie career. He had a small role in the film *Where the Day Takes You*. Unlike his TV show, the movie was serious. It is about homeless teens in Los Angeles. It looks at how they get by on the streets. Working on the film allowed Smith to learn from respected young actors such as Dermot Mulroney and Lara Flynn Boyle. Smith's role as

New role: Will had a small role in *Where the Day Takes You* with *(from left)* James Le Gros, Ricki Lake, Balthazar Getty, Dermot Mulroney, and Lara Flynn Boyle.

the wheelchair-bound Manny was a big change from his fun-loving character on TV. By taking on this tough part, Smith showed that he was serious about acting.

The movie wasn't a hit. But it was a good experience for Smith. His eyes opened not only to dramatic acting but also to homelessness. "Just seeing how people ignore the homeless was an amazing lesson," he said. "I was in full makeup on Hollywood Boulevard, and people didn't even know me. It was [surprising] seeing how cold people could be."

Homebase

In 1991, by the time Smith was twenty-two, his TV show was a hit. His movie career had begun. And he'd finally gotten himself out of debt. He and Jeff Townes were ready to celebrate by doing what they did best—making music.

The pair worked around Smith's busy schedule, writing and recording their next album, *Homebase*. With the album came new pressures. The success of *The Fresh Prince of Bel-Air* had made Smith a TV star. He had to prove to his fans that he hadn't forgotten about rap.

 Smith got the producers to let Jeff Townes have an ongoing role on *The Fresh Prince of Bel-Air*. Smith enjoyed having his friend around. But it was clear that Townes didn't have Smith's comfort in front of the camera.

Homebase, released in July 1991, didn't disappoint. Its rhymes were crisp and clean. They lacked some of the youthful silliness of earlier albums. But that was to be expected. Smith had grown up. He wasn't a kid anymore.

The album's biggest single was "Summertime." The song, about the joys of a summer day, got heavy radio play. The video became an

MTV favorite. After the letdown of *And in This Corner...*, the success of *Homebase* was a relief. Smith's acting career was taking off. But it wasn't yet time to write off music.

In September *The Fresh Prince of Bel-Air* entered its second season. Ratings kept climbing. Smith's acting had come a long way.

Meanwhile, Smith had fallen in love. Through a friend, he had met a fashion design student named Sheree Zampino. By December he had bought her an engagement ring. He proposed on Christmas Eve. She said yes. The couple began planning a May wedding.

In love: Will and Sheree attend the Emmy Awards in 1993.

Smith's schedule didn't leave much time for wedding plans. Taping of *The Fresh Prince of Bel-Air* continued. And the awards for *Homebase* started pouring in. Smith and Townes accepted a Grammy in February of 1992. Smith also won an Image Award from the National Association for the Advancement of Colored People (NAACP) for his music. In addition, *The Fresh Prince of Bel-Air* won an Image Award for Best Comedy Series.

Founded in 1909, the NAACP is a group that works to ensure equal rights for African Americans and all U.S. citizens.

If all of that wasn't enough, Smith soon learned that Zampino was pregnant. Smith wasn't going to be only a husband. He was also going to be a father. Smith was excited. But he knew that once the baby came, he'd have to cut back on work. He wanted to enjoy fatherhood.

Until then he planned to stay busy. One of his projects was a new movie. He took a part in *Made in America*. This comedy starred Ted Danson and Whoopi Goldberg. Smith played the boyfriend of one of the film's characters. Smith's film role was a lot like his TV character. But it was a bigger part than he'd had in *Where the Day Takes You*. It got the attention of movie producers. They were starting to see Smith as a box office draw.

Some wondered why Smith took small parts. After all, he was becoming a big star. Smith explained that he still had a lot to learn. "I'm still working on my acting skills," he said. "I feel I've improved, but I'm still not ready to step out with my own feature."

Leading Man

Next, Smith took on the role of Paul in the film *Six Degrees of Separation*. It was a huge step and his first starring role. Playing the lead was

New challenge: Will took on the role of Paul in *Six Degrees of Separation (above)*. Here he appears with costars Heather Graham and Eric Thal.

a challenge for someone new to acting. The role also gave Smith a big jump in pay. After earning fifty thousand dollars for his role in *Where the Day Takes You*, he got five hundred thousand dollars for *Six Degrees of Separation*.

Smith worked hard to earn that money. He changed the way he spoke. He worked out. He needed to look trim for the part. He did all he could to become the character he was playing.

"It was the first time I ever had to become someone else," he said. "All of your instincts and all the things that you've worked on, all the faces you learn to make and all your tools are stripped. . . . The role was so different from me that I had to adjust every aspect of myself to play it."

www.usatoday.com

USA TODAY

Life

SECTION D

December 8, 1993

Will Smith's exponential leap: *Six Degrees* elevates rapper and TV star

<u>From the Pages of USA TODAY</u>

There's a scene in *Six Degrees of Separation* where Will Smith—yes, that Will Smith—does a soliloquy on *Catcher in the Rye*. "Six straight, full, small-print, single-spaced pages of dialogue," says Smith, whose day job is starring in NBC's *The Fresh Prince of Bel-Air*. The speech, all done in one shot, was so demanding that "it almost made me not want to take the role."

But Smith, 25, is no dummy. The part is such a plum it will launch him as a film actor, even though he also had a dramatic role in last year's little-seen *Where the Day Takes You*.

Smith says he worked 18 weeks with both a dialect coach and an acting coach. When Smith became TV's Fresh Prince, he had no acting experience, but the show became a hit based largely on his charm. "I felt there was this big secret about acting that I didn't know." But after lessons, "it's all in what works for you."

Smith has been criticized because, though he plays a gay man in *Six Degrees*, he refused to kiss Anthony Michael Hall, insisting director Fred Schepisi fake the shot from behind. He knows that was a mistake. "I've seen the film. It shows. I've cheapened myself as an actor. . . . I spoke to Denzel Washington and he said if you're going to take a role, do what the role calls for. Basically it's what Mr. Miyagi told Daniel-san in *The Karate Kid*: `You karate do yes, you're OK; you karate do no, you're OK; you karate do maybe, squish like grape!'"

—Tom Green

Adding to the challenge, *Six Degrees of Separation* wasn't a comedy. The film is a drama about an African American con man (Smith) who tricks rich white families out of their money. The film deals with racism, homophobia (fear of gay people), and class bias. Smith hoped the role would make people take him more seriously as an actor.

But a problem soon emerged. In one scene, Smith's character was supposed to kiss another man. In an interview, Smith said he wasn't comfortable with the scene. He later refused to do it. The director had to film the scene another way. Smith's refusal angered some people. They thought he was being homophobic.

Smith later said that refusing to do the scene was a mistake. He felt he hadn't completely committed to his role. "If you're not going to commit, don't take [the part]," he said about the incident.

Smith's performance in *Six Degrees of Separation* got good reviews. *Entertainment Weekly* was impressed. So was the *Hollywood Reporter*. Not all the reviews praised him, though. The *New York Times*, for example, thought Smith's acting lacked passion. They didn't think he was a good fit for the part.

Return to the Prince
Smith had worked hard to prepare for his role in *Six Degrees of Separation*. He had a hard time leaving it behind. Turning back into the Fresh Prince was a challenge. To get back into character, he watched old episodes of the show. He even returned to Philadelphia to hang out with old friends.

With the baby due that winter, Smith was eager to return to his music. He might not have time for it once the baby came. So while *The Fresh Prince of Bel-Air* was filming its third season, he and Jeff Townes worked on their next album, titled *Code Red*.

Perhaps the duo were rushed as they worked on the album. Or maybe the rap scene had changed too much since *Homebase* had come out. Whatever the reason, *Code Red* was a flop. It sold just three hundred thousand copies. With Smith's fame, that figure was shockingly low. The poor sales pushed Smith in a direction he'd been headed for some time. He felt that it was time to leave rap behind for a while. With his acting career on the rise and a baby on the way, something had to go. Music seemed like the natural choice.

Willard C. Smith III was born in December 1992. His parents didn't want the baby to spend his life as a junior. So they agreed to call him Trey (another word for "three").

Smith was already thinking about the example he wanted to set. "When the doctor handed [Trey] to me, I realized things were different now," he said. "I have to wear my seat belt now and things like that—work out, stay healthy, eat right—because it's not just for me anymore."

Meanwhile, Smith was taking a more active role in *The Fresh Prince of Bel-Air*. He was helping more with script ideas. He even tried (and failed) to write a script of his own. Soon he wasn't just the star of the show. He also became the coproducer. He had a hand in planning the show. He pushed to include shows on serious issues,

IN FOCUS

Racism—Onscreen and Offscreen

The Fresh Prince of Bel-Air was a comedy. Most of the episodes were just fun. But the show also took on serious topics. One episode was based on an event from Smith's life. In the episode, a police officer pulled over Smith's character and his cousin for driving a nice car. Believing that two African American teenagers must have stolen the expensive vehicle, he put them in jail. A similar incident had happened to Smith shortly after he had become famous. A police officer hadn't believed he legally owned the Corvette he was driving.

such as sex and drugs. Like Smith off the set, the Fresh Prince was growing up.

Smith chose not to take on a movie role when filming for the third season was finished. He'd been tempted by the role of Robin in the blockbuster *Batman Returns*. But the role had gone to another actor. So Smith stayed home. He spent time being a dad and getting ready for the next season of *The Fresh Prince of Bel-Air*. He also knew he needed to spend time with his wife. With his busy schedule and a baby, the couple had been having trouble making time for each other. Together, they bought a house in Thousand Oaks, California, and teamed up to decorate it.

By the time the fourth season started in 1993, Smith had taken on the title of executive producer. In this role, he had more say about the show than ever before. He continued to push for serious episodes. Smith wanted the show to reach people in meaningful ways. Comedy was great. But he also wanted something of impact. That desire was another sign of his growth. He had become a father. The days of carefree fun were over.

Bad Boys: Will costarred with Martin Lawrence *(left)* in *Bad Boys* in 1994. *Bad Boys* is about two police officers investigating the drug trade in Los Angeles.

Action Star

In 1994 Smith's film career took another leap. Don Simpson and Jerry Bruckheimer sent him a script for a movie called *Bad Boys*. The producers had been successful with *Beverly Hills Cop*, a blend of comedy and action that had starred Eddie Murphy. Many people compared Smith to a young Murphy. So Smith seemed a perfect fit for *Bad Boys*. With a $2 million offer on the table, he took the part. His costar in the movie was another rising actor named Martin Lawrence.

www.usatoday.com

USA TODAY

Life

SECTION D

April 11, 1995

Action heroes pack a comedy punch

<u>From the Pages of</u>
<u>USA TODAY</u>

Where's the action? Judging from this weekend's box-office returns, it's with *Bad Boys*, the Martin Lawrence-Will Smith action-comedy, which opened with a bang, taking in $15.5 million, the largest opening of the year. The film's explosive take could put its two comic stars where Beverly Hills Cop put Eddie Murphy a decade ago.

"Martin and Will taking Eddie Murphy's place?" Smith marvels. "Hey, no way we could be compared to him after just one movie," Adds Lawrence, "When I think about action heroes, I go right to the top ones: Schwarzenegger, Willis. I hadn't imagined myself playing that role."

Still, the pair had the prerequisites for roles that blend ha-ha with bang-bang.

"You've got to have presence, you've got to have physicality—but you've also got to be able to act," says *Bad Boys* producer Don Simpson. "Otherwise you're just a stick figure with big muscles. But Will and Martin—it's like one plus one equals 10."

—Marshall Fine

The pair hit it off. "When I met [Smith], there was an instant chemistry between us," Lawrence said. "I knew if we could get that chemistry on camera, we'd be cool. We opened our hearts to each other and decided we could be partners."

Friends on and off the screen, the two men worked out for their roles. *Bad Boys* would be an action movie with physically demanding scenes. Smith had played in a comic role and a dramatic role. Action was a new direction.

As filming got started, the chemistry between the stars was obvious. They loved to play off each other and ad-lib (make up new lines). Director Michael Bay encouraged them. The resulting humor was a big part of the film's success.

For the most part, critics hated the movie. They said it wasn't original. They thought the dialog was weak. But even many critics who disliked the movie praised Smith and Lawrence. *Rolling Stone* magazine said, "It's all special effects noise and nonsense, but we're not fooled. Lawrence and Smith are the real firecrackers."

The actors took the film's bad reviews in stride. Many action movies strike out with critics. What matters is the fans. And people flocked to see *Bad Boys*. The movie took in more than $15 million the first weekend. It went on to make more than $140 million worldwide. Those were big numbers. Suddenly movie producers were looking at Smith in a new light.

Changes

That fall, Smith returned to the set of *The Fresh Prince of Bel-Air* for the show's fifth season. By this time, he was growing tired of the sitcom. He would have liked to focus on movies full-time. But he agreed to honor his contract with NBC. That meant he had two more seasons to shoot.

The first new episode of the season was the show's one-hundredth. One hundred episodes is a milestone for any sitcom. Typically with that number, a show can go into syndication. That means old episodes can be sold directly to any TV station and run at any time. These sales can create big profits (called royalties) for the actors and producers. With such a big role in the show, Smith could make a lot of money in royalties. To celebrate, the show aired a full hour instead of the usual half hour. After the airing, the cast and crew went to a party in Los Angeles.

The party was fun. But Smith was looking ahead to bigger things. He worked hard to improve the show. But at the end of the year, he told NBC that the 1995–1996 season would be his last. He'd done all he could with his character.

"It's like leaving a family, more than just leaving a job," he said of the choice. "But creatively, I was starting to feel [bored]. There wasn't anywhere to go. I had seen how vast the film world could be. You can do anything on a big screen, there's so much more room. That was more exciting."

Change was coming in Smith's personal life too. Problems came up at home and didn't go away. Smith and his wife loved their son. But the romance between them was gone. The couple decided to separate. Later, they divorced. Smith stayed positive through it all. He'd experienced divorce when his parents' marriage had ended. He wanted his own divorce to go as smoothly as theirs had. Little Trey would live with his mother. But Smith would remain active in his life. The former couple remained friends, knowing that was best for their son.

Father and son: Will holds his son Trey in 1995.

In the summer of 1995, Smith took on the role that would establish him as one of Hollywood's biggest stars. As Air Force pilot Steven Hiller, he would be a hero in the science fiction thriller *Independence Day. Independence Day* was a big-budget event. Recent science fiction films such as *Jurassic Park* had set box office records. The movie studio 20th Century Fox was banking on *Independence Day* to be the latest science fiction blockbuster. Smith's star power would be a big factor.

"It was one of those projects that comes along once in a career," Smith said. "It has everything. You laugh, you cry . . . it has everything you could want from a movie. I'm also probably the first black guy to ever save the world."

The role appealed to Smith for more reasons than the budget. He'd always been a science fiction fan. *Independence Day*'s plot about alien invaders suited him. In addition, the role of Hiller wasn't written for an African American man, as Smith's previous roles had been. It was

To new heights: Will's role in *Independence Day* helped his career and the movie.

Blue-Screen Acting

For many of his movies, Smith has had to do what is called blue-screen acting. Actors play their parts in front of a huge screen instead of at a location. This screen is often blue. (That's where the term *blue screen* comes from.) But the screen can also be other colors, such as green *(below)* or red.

In blue-screen acting, actors often have to imagine other characters around them. Later, computers can take the footage and add in artificial characters and locations behind the actors. Blue-screen acting can be difficult. But the special effects that result are often fantastic.

a role that an actor of any race could have played, and he'd gotten it. Best of all, it was the perfect part to cement his place in Hollywood as an action star. Fighting aliens and dodging explosions—that was the stuff of an action hero.

That summer Smith filmed some of the most memorable scenes of his career. The cast and crew went to Utah's Bonneville Salt Flats.

Won't forget: The Bonneville Salt Flats provided a memorable backdrop for some of Will's scenes in *Independence Day*.

There, they filmed a scene in which Hiller fights an alien and drags it across the desert. Smith had to battle heat near 120°F (49°C). Worse still, he was acting alone. Computers would add in the alien later.

"If you're acting with an alien, it's a mark on the floor or some-thing," Smith said. "And it's [filmed] in such small pieces that you can never really get a good run at a scene. . . . But what's fun about doing a science fiction movie is when you finally see everything put together, it's almost as if you weren't even there. It looks completely different."

With *Independence Day*'s special effects yet to be added, it would be almost a year before it appeared in theaters. Smith and the rest of the cast had to get on with their careers while they waited. So with filming complete, Smith returned for the last season of *The Fresh Prince of Bel-Air*.

July 8, 1996

Will Smith flying high

From the Pages of
USA TODAY

Will Smith may be starring in the box office monster *Independence Day*, but right now he just wants to talk about . . . Ernest Borgnine? Smith, hanging at Essex House hotel on Central Park South, says that the portly character actor inspired him while he was grappling with his fighter pilot role in the new alien invasion thriller.

"Ernest Borgnine's character was the only character in *The Poseidon Adventure* that was funny," says Smith. "And it's a weird thing, because it's not comedy," he adds. "It's just funny. I was really struggling with that, and Ernest Borgnine was the character that really got me on track."

As Capt. Steven Hiller, Smith is believable but outrageous. In his signature moment, he punches an alien in the face, quipping: 'Welcome to Earth.' "Those lines are dangerous because they can be corny," Smith says. "You've got to find the delivery so that the audiences feel like that's what they would have wanted to say."

Smith has also found the secret to ingratiating himself with his coworkers. "Will Smith is one of the great joys I've ever had as a filmmaker," says *Independence Day* writer-producer Dean Devlin. "He's been so successful so long, but he's kind to everybody on the set," says costar Jeff Goldblum.

"What *The Fresh Prince of Bel-Air* taught me is that there's this perfect work zone between tension and lollygagging," he says. "The more fun that you have, the more you're going to get accomplished." Smith knows he has reached a new level in his career. He's kissing the Fresh Prince character good-bye. "It was difficult to leave the show, but I wanted to go out right—when I wanted to, with them begging me to do another season—rather than being thrown out."

—Andy Seiler

New love: Will began dating Jada Pinkett in 1995.

Rise to the Top

In the fall of 1995, Smith's personal life changed again. He began to have romantic feelings for actress Jada Pinkett. The two had been friends for a long time. Five years before, Pinkett had tried out to play Smith's girlfriend on the TV show. Producers had decided that the 5-foot (1.5 m) actress wasn't tall enough to play the Fresh Prince's love interest. That limitation didn't stop Pinkett from becoming Smith's real-life love interest. Like Smith, Pinkett was coming out of a relationship (with NBA star

Grant Hill). Smith and Pinkett comforted each other and talked. At some point, they fell in love.

"I helped him understand what happened in his marriage, and he helped me see what happened in my relationship," Pinkett said. "He's become my best friend. There's nothing I can't say to him, nothing I can't share."

Smith said he was surprised by his feelings. "You don't know about all the walls you build up in your mind and heart until someone comes along and tears them down," he said.

Soon the twenty-seven-year-old Smith and the twenty-four-year-old Pinkett were spending all their free time together. Tabloids loved to run stories about the couple. Photographers loved to snap their picture. But despite the unwanted attention, Smith was happy. His run as the Fresh Prince was coming to a welcome end. His movie career was taking off. And best of all, he was in love. Life was good.

In March of 1996, Smith and the rest of the cast taped the 149th—and final—episode of *The Fresh Prince of Bel-Air*. After the taping, the cast gathered for a farewell party. The show's end left Smith both sad and excited. The show would go on in syndication. But an important chapter in Smith's life was over.

Out on the town: Will and Jada Pinkett attend the Academy Awards, or Oscars, in 1996.

"When I started doing *The Fresh Prince of Bel-Air*, I was twenty years old," Smith said. "Inside those years, I went through three careers, music, television, movies. I got married, had a baby, divorced. It's like I did a whole lot of living in that time. My life experiences are so far advanced beyond the character's life experiences. It was almost like [stepping back] for me to play that character."

A few months later, on July 4, *Independence Day* finally opened. It was a hit. Despite going up against *Mission Impossible* and several other big films, *Independence Day* ruled the box office. It took in more than $50 million in its opening weekend. Within months it soared to the $300 million mark. No more doubts existed about Smith's box office appeal. The film also got good reviews. Critics compared it to science fiction classics from the 1950s. They praised Smith for his ability to make Hiller both serious and funny.

Man in Black

While *Independence Day* was wowing fans, Smith was already working on his next role. He wouldn't normally have chosen to do another science fiction film right away. But when director and producer Steven Spielberg called him about a science fiction comedy called *Men in Black*, Smith couldn't refuse. Spielberg was so successful that Smith jumped at the chance to work with him. The $5 million he was offered to take the part didn't hurt either.

> When Steven Spielberg first called Smith about *Men in Black*, Smith thought it was someone playing a joke on him.

Smith costarred with Academy Award-winner Tommy Lee Jones in the film. They play a pair of secret agents in charge of tracking aliens secretly living on Earth. The role allowed Smith to return to his comedic roots. But it also offered plenty of action. The studio (Columbia) heavily promoted the film, allowing Smith to remain in the public eye.

The serious Jones and the lighthearted Smith made a great pair. The actors' on-screen chemistry was clear. As Agent J, Smith was careful not to re-create his character from *Independence Day*. A danger to any actor's career is being typecast. An actor who plays too many similar roles can get stuck in a mold. Producers and directors have a hard time seeing them in roles that differ from their norm. From the start of his acting career, Smith had made a point of learning from the actors he worked with. The Oscar-winning Jones was no exception.

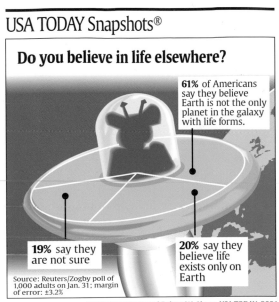

USA TODAY Snapshots®

Do you believe in life elsewhere?

61% of Americans say they believe Earth is not the only planet in the galaxy with life forms.

19% say they are not sure

20% say they believe life exists only on Earth

Source: Reuters/Zogby poll of 1,000 adults on Jan. 31; margin of error: ±3.2%

By William Risser and Robert W. Ahren, USA TODAY, 2001

"He knows everything that's going on on the set," Smith said of his costar. "The lights and the cameras, he knows how everything works, in order to put himself in a position to have his greatness captured."

Jones wasn't the only actor who was praised for his work on the set. Smith impressed director Barry Sonnenfeld. "Will on the set is incredibly relaxed, self-confident, and at ease with himself," he said. "He's always energetic, bouncing on his toes. He's just got too much energy."

Men in Black opened on July 4, 1997. It got great reviews. Good reviews and heavy promotion made the film another summer

Taking direction: Will and Tommy Lee Jones *(center)* talk with director Barry Sonnenfeld on the set of *Men in Black*.

blockbuster. *Men in Black* took in more than $80 million in its first week. It went on to make almost $600 million worldwide.

Big Willie

Smith wasn't just cool on the screen. He also wrote and recorded a rap, "Men in Black," to serve as the movie's theme. The rap played as the closing credits rolled. It topped the Billboard Hot 100 Singles Airplay chart for weeks. This chart lists the 100 songs that play most often on the radio. The video for the song earned Smith the MTV Video Music Award for Best Video from a Film.

Smith followed up the success of the single with his first full-length solo album. Titled *Big Willie Style*, the album included "Men in Black" as well as the hit "Gettin' Jiggy Wit It." Smith's album sold more than four million copies within a year. "Gettin' Jiggy Wit It" spent two weeks on

wants to have a baby but doesn't want to marry. So she hires a man (Smith) to father the child without becoming attached. But along the way, the two fall in love. Smith and Pinkett sold the idea to Universal. The studio was eager to make a movie featuring one of Hollywood's hottest couples.

Everything was going so well that Smith proposed. In November 1997, the couple announced their engagement. On New Year's Eve, they married in a small ceremony near Pinkett's hometown of Baltimore, Maryland. Pinkett worked with designers to plan the lavish

wedding. With hundreds of candles and flowers, velvet drapery, and more, the wedding reportedly cost more than $3 million. The couple wrote their own vows.

They read them before about 125 guests. After the ceremony, they celebrated with food and music. Smith even got onstage to perform for the guests. The good news didn't stop there, either. Shortly after the wedding, the couple announced that they were going to have a baby.

I do: Will and Jada smile as they walk down the aisle on their wedding day, December 31, 1997.

Enemy of the State

The couple would have liked to start work on *Love for Sale*. But Pinkett's pregnancy and Smith's other projects caused them to put it off. The first of Smith's new projects was the action-thriller *Enemy of the State*. His role earned him $14 million. He played Robert Clayton Dean, a man whose life falls apart when his identity is stolen.

Once again, Smith had a chance to work with a well-respected actor—Gene Hackman. But Smith couldn't rely too much on his co-star. This wasn't a "buddy film." Smith was on his own for most of the scenes. He quickly learned how demanding that made the role.

"It's the first time that I've been completely out front, where the story is about my character," he said. "It's not just physically [tiring]. The emotional aspect can be equally [tough]."

The film was another big step in Smith's career. He was performing in a purely dramatic role. After a pair of blockbuster science fiction films, he wanted to prove that he could go in a different direction. But despite the strong cast and action-filled plot, *Enemy of the State* was only a mild success. The film drew mixed reviews. And it didn't have the box office appeal of Smith's earlier blockbusters.

Dynamic trio: Will poses with *Enemy of the State* costars Gene Hackman *(left)* and Jon Voight at the premiere in 1998.

The film's modest success didn't slow the demand for Smith, though. He was quickly joining actors such as Tom Hanks and Tom Cruise as one of Hollywood's most sought-after leading men. Along with Denzel Washington, he was the industry's leading African American star. He was getting big, race-neutral roles. His talent was becoming well known.

Between 1997 and 2008, Tom Hanks had a leading role in twelve films with an average salary of $20.5 million. Tom Cruise averaged $33 million per film for his eleven leading roles. Denzel Washington made $16.4 million per picture for his sixteen films. And Will appeared in the lead in thirteen films for an average of $18.7 million per picture.

Smith knew that being a top African American actor put him in a position to impact people. "There is definitely a burden to carry," he said. "But I think that responsibility has always made blacks that choose to carry the burden stronger. I want to play positive characters. I want to play characters that represent really strong, positive black images."

A Wild Disaster

In 1998 Barry Sonnenfeld contacted Smith about a project called *Wild Wild West*. Sonnenfeld had liked working with Smith on *Men in Black*. He wanted to team up again. "Once you work with [Smith]," he said, "you want to work with him forever."

Because of the success they'd shared with *Men in Black*, Smith agreed to play the role of cowboy Jim West. He was comfortable with Sonnenfeld, who assured him that *Wild Wild West* would be another blockbuster. The idea of playing an African American cowboy in the strange western also appealed to Smith. *Wild Wild West* is based on a 1960s TV show. It features over-the-top gadgets and vehicles. It plays like a James Bond movie set in the Old West. Smith even uses a famous Bond line in the film, introducing himself as "West . . . Jim West."

Smith's faith in Sonnenfeld led him to turn down another science fiction blockbuster. He declined the role of Neo in the movie *The Matrix* because he'd be busy with *Wild Wild West*. Smith couldn't have

IN F⊕CUS

A Missed Opportunity

The role of Neo in *The Matrix*, which Smith turned down, went to actor Keanu Reeves. The movie, about a superhuman man (Reeves) in a virtual world, was a huge hit. *The Matrix* went on to gross almost $740 million worldwide, more than any of Smith's movies. Two successful sequels followed. The three films were a big boost to Reeves's career.

Matrix 2: *(from left)* Will's wife Jada, Laurence Fishburne, Carrie-Anne Moss, and Keanu Reeves starred in the second Matrix movie, *The Matrix Revolutions.*

Family affair: Jada with Jaden and Will with Trey pose in cowboy outfits at the Los Angeles premiere of *Wild Wild West* in 1999.

known it at the time, but *The Matrix* would go on to become one of the most popular science fiction movies of all time. He would later call the decision one of the biggest mistakes of his career.

But at the time, Smith believed he had a hit with *Wild Wild West*. The film is full of humor and special effects. Its cast includes popular stars Kevin Kline and Salma Hayek. It was a similar formula to what Smith and Sonnenfeld had done with *Men in Black*. Everything seemed to be in place. Smith even recorded the film's theme song, "Wild Wild West."

As with most films, a long wait took place between filming and release. During this time, Pinkett gave birth to a baby boy. The couple named him Jaden. The birth of his second child only inspired Smith to work harder.

The song and video for "Wild Wild West" came out before the film in the summer of 1999. With a catchy tune and movie scenes in the video, it was a hit. The song's success, along with heavy promotion from the film studio, built up big expectations for the latest Will Smith feature.

But the film couldn't match the success of the song. Despite a good opening week of about $50 million, the film got bad reviews. The *Washington Post* mocked the movie by calling it Wild Wild Waste. The reviewer called it a waste of time, money, and talent.

When he saw the finished product, Smith understood. It wasn't a good movie. No amount of special effects could save it. As critics ripped it and audiences avoided it, Smith was embarrassed. He felt he'd let down his fans.

Critics kept piling it on. The Razzies—a set of joke awards given out to the worst movies of the year—named *Wild Wild West* 1999's worst movie. They also gave the film "awards" for worst screenplay, worst song, worst director, and worst screen couple (Smith and Kline). It was official. *Wild Wild West* was Smith's first big-screen flop.

Back on His Feet

It wasn't all bad news for Smith, though. In 1999 he won another Grammy award. This time the honor was for his song "Gettin' Jiggy Wit It."

Smith also released another album that year. Smith produced the album himself, with the help of Jeff Townes.

Best rap solo performance: Will took home another Grammy in 1999.

November 16, 1999

Will Smith still gets the last laugh

From the Pages of
USA TODAY

Probably nobody in hip-hop has been "playa hated" longer than Will Smith. Long before his sitcoms and movies, the rapper heard he wasn't hard-core enough to be taken seriously. Perhaps that's why he spouts his trademark "ha-ha, ha-ha" with such relish or gleefully boasts that he's "soft as in Microsoft." The fact is, he can rhyme and is never dull, even if there's nothing gritty or deep about what he has to say. He dares fellow MCs to "write one verse without a curse," and even the raunchy Lil' Kim (who guests on *Da Butta*) keeps it clean for the Jiggiest One. When he's not rapping about how large he has gotten, he spends time talking about family and loyalty. Longtime collaborator Jazzy Jeff is all over the record and even puts on a turntable-scratching exhibition for old times' sake. Biz Markie and Slick Rick bring some old-school flavor and humor to *So Fresh*, and Eve matches Smith line for line on *Can You Feel Me?*

—Steve Jones

Released in November 1999, *Willennium* was Smith's second full-length solo album. The album title was a play on the word *millennium*. This refers to a period of one thousand years. In 2000, people would celebrate the arrival of a new millennium. The album's biggest single, "Will2K," also played on the upcoming new year. The term *2k* means "2,000." "Will2K" made Billboard's top ten. It also earned Smith another Grammy nomination for Best Music Video, Short Form.

After living through the criticism of *Wild Wild West*, Smith was ready for a quieter role. He found it in *The Legend of Bagger Vance*, directed by Robert Redford. Despite the film's title, Smith's role as mystical golf caddy Bagger Vance wasn't the lead. That role went to Matt Damon. The film was an unusual choice for Smith and not just because he had a supporting part. The character of Vance is soft spoken and wise. For the first time, Smith played a mature role. After the flop of *Wild Wild West*, it seemed to be the perfect part to reestablish himself as a dramatic actor.

But the choice again left Smith open to criticism. Many critics found the movie's plot silly. Smith's character annoyed the critics,

New direction: *(from right)* Robert Redford gives J. Michael Moncrief, Will, and Matt Damon a golf lesson for *Bagger Vance*.

though more for how the part was written than for how Smith played it. Criticism also came from Spike Lee, an African American director Smith respected. He questioned Smith for taking a role that ignored the plight of African Americans during the 1930s (the period in which the film was set).

For years it had seemed as if Smith could do no wrong. Suddenly, it seemed as if he wasn't doing anything right. He was a bona fide star. But many believed he wasn't living up to the high expectations he'd set for himself. With his reputation suffering, Smith had work to do.

Living legend: Will applauds legend Muhammad Ali after presenting the boxer with an award at the Black Entertainment Television (BET) Awards in 2002.

The Role of a Lifetime

Since his early days in film, Smith had measured himself against other TV stars who had gone on to make movies. Many actors try to make the jump. Most fail. But some manage to carve out good careers in film. A few become great dramatic actors. Two such actors were Tom Hanks and Jim Carrey. Both started out as TV comics. Like Smith, Hanks had gotten his acting break with a sitcom—*Bosom*

Buddies. Carrey, meanwhile, had made his name on the late-night comedy *In Living Color.*

Both of these actors had needed that one special role to change the perception of them as TV stars. For Hanks it was as AIDS patient Andrew Beckett in *Philadelphia.* In 1993 Hanks won an Oscar for the performance. Carrey's breakthrough role was as Andy Kaufman in *Man on the Moon.* Carrey wasn't nominated for an Oscar for the role. But many felt that he should have been.

Footsteps to follow: Both Jim Carrey *(left)* and Tom Hanks *(right)* started on television comedies and moved on to comedic and dramatic movies.

By late 2000, Smith was thirty-two years old. He was the father of three children. (Pinkett had given birth to a girl named Willow in October of that year.) He was a respected actor and an action star. But nobody thought of him as a top dramatic actor. He just wasn't the sort of actor who earned Oscar consideration. That changed when he agreed to play boxing legend Muhammad Ali in the upcoming film *Ali.*

Muhammad Ali

Cassius Clay was born in Kentucky in 1942. He began boxing at an early age and turned professional in 1960. Over the next three years, he built up a 19–0 record. In 1964 he beat Sonny Liston to become the heavyweight champion of the world.

Clay made the news for more than just boxing, though. Soon he announced that he had joined the Nation of Islam. The Nation of Islam is an African American religious group known for its political beliefs. The group practices a form of Islam. Clay changed his name to Muhammad Ali. In 1966 he refused to serve in the Vietnam War (1957–1975) and was stripped of his boxing title. He wasn't allowed to box in the United States again until 1970. Ali went on to participate in many famous fights. He became one of the best-known boxers of all time.

Fighting shape: Muhammad Ali takes a shot at a bag in 1999.

Becoming Ali

Columbia/Sony Pictures had long planned to make a film about the life of Ali. Born Cassius Clay, the boxer was more than just a sports hero. He was a political icon and a symbol of the strife of the 1960s and 1970s. In those decades, African Americans were fighting for equal rights. Playing such a complex man would be the biggest challenge of Smith's career. Sony had asked him before. But it wasn't until 2000 that Smith felt ready to take on the role.

A big reason he decided to do the film was a phone call he got from Ali. "I was about to turn it down," Smith said. "Then [Ali] called me himself. He said, 'You are almost pretty enough to play me.' He told me that his family [was] involved in the script and that he wanted [the film] to be a tribute to his life. That conversation took a lot of pressure away from me."

USA TODAY Snapshots

You ought to be in pictures

Sports celebrities that people[1] would most like to be photographed with:

Muhammad Ali	24%
Shaquille O'Neal	23%
Tiger Woods	23%
Alex Rodriguez	13%
Wayne Gretzky	9%
Tom Brady	8%

1 – More than 37,000 respondents were surveyed
Source: *Popular Photography & Imaging* and America Online

By Ellen J. Horrow and Alejandro Gonzalez, USA TODAY, 2004

Joking around: Muhammad Ali jokes with Will at the first showing of *Ali*.

Playing Ali would require more work than any role Smith had played. First, he had to bulk up. Already strong, Smith had to add even more muscle to look like Ali. He started working out. He ran in heavy boots, lifted weights, and even took boxing lessons.

Getting physically ready wasn't the end of it. Because Ali was so well known, Smith had to study the man. He wanted to talk like Ali, move like Ali, and even think like Ali. He watched videotapes of Ali in

www.usatoday.com

USA TODAY

Life

SECTION D

December 21, 2001

Will Smith, the greatest: Taking on the legendary Muhammad Ali

<u>From the Pages of</u>
<u>USA TODAY</u>

The actor recalls the danger, the palpable threat of imminent pain, the unnerving helplessness. At that millisecond, self-preservation was his best friend. Reflexively, the novice fighter in him protectively tucked his chin. Too late. A leather-encased hammer, disguised as a fist, jarred him upside his elegantly shaped head.

A bona fide heavyweight got fresh with the would-be boxing prince, transforming the actor's slinky neck into a reluctant shock absorber and transmitting shock waves through his central nervous system. This was Hollywood, wasn't it? He was making a movie, wasn't he? Well, yes and no. It was make-believe. But this was not acting. Will Smith was becoming Muhammad Ali. The hard way.

"I felt an electric shock from the base of my neck down to the back of both elbows, like someone had touched my spine with an electrical cord," says Smith, and out of the boxing ring. He read books about him. He even studied Nation of Islam, a religious group Ali belonged to.

One of the most memorable moments of Smith's preparation was when he got into the ring to fight a professional boxer. The pro knocked Smith out. "There was a bright blue flash that faded to black," Smith remembered. "I don't know how to describe it, but there was the sound—whooo-ohhh-whoo."

sipping black coffee. "Have you ever put your tongue on a 9-volt battery? That was the taste I had in my mouth. There was a bright blue flash that faded to black."

Smith is the outrageously charismatic, boyishly imperfect, graceful, naive and sexually provocative Ali, a planet of ambivalence orbiting in a galaxy of scheming sycophants—benevolent to mankind, yet capable of brutally punishing a human being for refusing to call him by his Muslim name.

The portrayal was a serious challenge for the 33 year old actor. For the former Grammy-winning rapper and sitcom star, this is a major departure from his breakthrough film role in *Six Degrees of Separation* to the blockbusters *Independence Day* and *Men in Black*. Smith's last effort, *The Legend of Bagger Vance*, was flattened at the box office.

Smith is beginning to get recognition for *Ali*, but the film itself continues to be snubbed by critics and movie industry award lists. On Thursday, the Golden Globe Awards bestowed only acting nominations to Smith and Jon Voight, who plays sports broadcaster Howard Cosell.

Playing an American icon, and perhaps the world's most recognizable personality, was daunting and illuminating. "That was part of the bittersweet nature of this role—to be able to study, define and try to quantify greatness, to wear the robe of greatness as an actor, but to potentially never know if I possessed that greatness for real," Smith says. "I've been to my physical, mental, emotional, spiritual and financial limits. I know who I am now. And this film made it more transparent to me who I want to be."

—Jon Saraceno

(i) Muhammad Ali's daughter Laila praised Smith's acting skills. But when she heard that Smith was going to take on a professional fighter, she could only laugh. Laila, a boxer herself, said that Smith had no idea what being hit was really like.

When he read the script, Smith realized he'd have his first love scene. But his worries about the scene disappeared when Pinkett got the part of Ali's wife. The couple was excited about the chance to work together.

With the long filming process nearly over, director Michael Mann wanted to go to Africa to film the movie's final scenes. They center on one of Ali's most famous fights, often called the Rumble in the Jungle. But there was a problem with Mann's plan. The trip would be expensive. The film was already over budget. Sony feared that paying for the trip would put the company at risk to lose money. The producers told Mann to film the scenes without going to Africa.

Smith and Mann talked about the problem. They agreed that the scenes needed to be filmed in Africa. Smith badly wanted the movie to

IN F◉CUS

The Ear Problem

For his role as Ali, Smith did everything he could to look, sound, and act like the boxer. But there was one problem. His ears stuck out farther than Ali's did. The solution was a special mold that held Smith's ears closer to his head. The mold took about an hour and a half to put on each day. Smith also had to wear a hairpiece. It covered Smith's forehead, which is larger than Ali's.

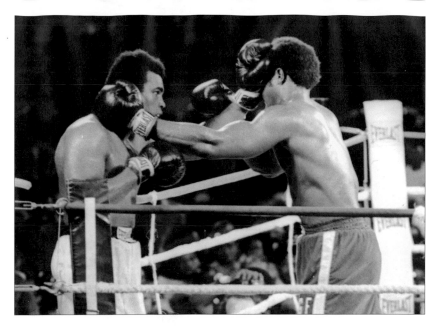

Rumble in the Jungle: In Zaire (later named Democratic Republic of Congo), Ali *(left)* fought George Foreman *(right).*

be a success. So he put up his own salary as a guarantee to Sony. If *Ali* lost money, they could take the losses out of his paycheck. Mann followed Smith's lead and made the same offer. It was a big risk for Smith, whose contract called for him to be paid $20 million.

The cast and crew flew to Mozambique, in southeastern Africa. It was Smith's first trip to Africa. What he saw there affected him deeply. The people he met gave him a warm welcome. He was shocked by how many of them knew of him. Even in this faraway country, people knew the name Will Smith. They even wanted to be in his movie.

For the movie's big scene—the fight—more than sixty-five thousand Mozambicans showed up to serve as extras in the crowd.

After the final day of shooting, Smith was playing with a group of children. They were dancing and singing. The kids even picked Smith up and carried him through the streets. Smith was deeply moved.

"It was weird," he said. "I didn't feel like they were carrying me because I was famous. It just felt like we had connected in some emotional way, in some way that was really spiritual. It gave me a great sense of what Ali must have felt the first time he came to Africa. It really inspired me."

In the moment: Will's trip to Africa helped him understand his character even more. This shot from *Ali* shows Will as Ali during a boxing match.

Reaction to *Ali*

Released on December 25, 2001, *Ali* took in more than $10 million on its first day. It broke box office records for Christmas Day. Smith's performance drew praise. But many critics disliked the way Mann had handled the film. They said that it moved slowly and made Ali's life seem almost boring.

December 14, 2001

Ali stars at *Ali* premiere

From the Pages of
USA TODAY

When is the star not the biggest draw at his own movie premiere? When the film is *Ali* and Muhammad Ali himself is on hand. That's how it was Wednesday, which was fine with Will Smith, who plays the world's most recognizable man in the biopic opening Christmas Day. "I will play second fiddle to Ali for the rest of my life," said Smith, with wife Jada Pinkett Smith (who plays Ali's first wife, Sonji, in the film), and sons Trey, 9, and Jaden, 3. "If I could only be second, if I could only get to second with Ali, that would be great."

Celebs from movies, music, politics and sports turned out, including Russell Crowe, Billy Crystal, Samuel L. Jackson, Eddie Murphy, Quincy Jones, Lionel Richie, Sisqo, Jesse Jackson, Jim Brown, Bruce Jenner, Magic Johnson, Sugar Ray Leonard, Lennox Lewis, Joe Namath and Dave Winfield. Fans, seated in the bleachers on the closed-off Hollywood Boulevard, shouted "Ah-lee! Ah-lee!" when The Greatest arrived with fifth wife Lonnie and two of his daughters, Laila, 23, a professional fighter, and Hana, 25.

The cast was thrilled to see the former heavyweight champ, who entertained them during filming. "He was walking around the set with Jon Voight's wig on for Howard Cosell making people laugh," said Nona Gaye, who plays Ali's second wife, Belinda. "He's still a funny guy and sharp as a tack."

Smith and Ali, 59, even exchanged light jabs on the red carpet. "You better hold me back," Smith said playfully. "I'm going to get you, champ." Smith, who bulked up for the role, is still holding onto a lot of that muscle. "I've been slipping a little bit," he said. "I love sparring, so it will probably be around for a while."

—Kelly Carter

That criticism didn't diminish Smith's performance, though. He'd never been the sort of actor to get Oscar consideration. But for his role in *Ali*, his peers nominated him for Best Actor. He also received a Golden Globe nomination.

IN FOCUS

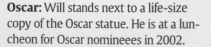

The Academy Awards

The Academy Awards are the most famous film awards in the world. The members of the Academy of Motion Picture Arts and Sciences vote on the many awards. The members first release nominations for the awards in each category. They then vote on the winners, who are honored in a fancy ceremony each year. The Oscar itself is a small gold statue. The statue is a knight holding a sword while standing on top of a reel of film.

Oscar: Will stands next to a life-size copy of the Oscar statue. He is at a luncheon for Oscar nomineees in 2002.

At the Oscars, Smith was up against stiff competition. Other nominees included Sean Penn for *I Am Sam*, Russell Crowe for *A Beautiful Mind*, Tom Wilkinson for *In the Bedroom*, and Denzel Washington for *Training Day*. "If this was the rap category at the Grammys, I'd feel like I have a much better shot," Smith joked. "I don't care who wins. I am completely honored to be in the company in this category."

Denzel Washington ended up winning the Oscar. Smith would have liked to win. But just being recognized was a huge step. He felt he had the respect of his peers. With the nomination, Smith could be sure that people didn't just see him as the Fresh Prince anymore. He was Will Smith, Oscar-nominated actor. And even though he didn't win the Oscar, his role in *Ali* did earn him a few honors. At the Black Entertainment Television Awards, he won Best Actor. At the MTV Movie Awards, he won for Best Male Performance.

Red carpet: Will and Jada walk the red carpet at the 2002 Academy Awards. Will was nominated for Best Actor for his portrayal of Muhammad Ali in *Ali*.

At the top: Fans surround Will. He is going to the first showing of *I, Robot* in Paris, France, in 2004.

Will Smith, Superstar

■■■■

Between the filming and release of *Ali*, Smith prepared for a pair of familiar roles. He had agreed to do sequels for two of his most popular movies—*Men in Black* and *Bad Boys*. The first of the two projects, *Men in Black II*, reunited him with Barry Sonnenfeld for the first time since their *Wild Wild West* disaster. The pair was eager to regain the public's trust.

Men in Black II had plenty of action and special effects. The film brought back the popular team of Smith and Tommy Lee Jones and took in more than $440 million worldwide. As with most sequels, *Men in Black II* didn't reach the heights of the original. It didn't get the same glowing reviews either. But fans liked it. And it helped Smith get over the letdown of *Wild Wild West*.

Bad Boys II was in many ways similar to *Men in Black II*. Smith got the same fee for both movies—$20 million. Both were sequels reuniting two stars—this time Smith and Martin Lawrence. And like *Men in Black II*, *Bad Boys II* found success by giving fans what they expected. Critics, however, hated the movie. *Rolling Stone* even compared it to toxic waste.

Castmates: *(from left)* Rosario Dawson, Will, Lara Flynn Boyle, and Tommy Lee Jones pose for a photo to promote *Men in Black II*.

www.usatoday.com

USA TODAY
Life
SECTION D

June 25, 2002

Will Smith commands rap attention with new 'Reign'

From the Pages of USA TODAY

As a rapper, Will Smith often has taken shots for not being hard-core like his more thuggish colleagues. But on his new *Born to Reign* album (* * * out of four), he has no problem reminding them who's the jiggiest of them all. Who else has had the president of the United States raising the roof and picks up an Oscar nomination? Who could challenge him at the top of the box office rankings when *Men in Black II* opens?

Smith basically keeps it clean and comedic, though he hasn't lost his penchant for flipping clever verses. He's like the classroom cut-up who fooled them all, and he never misses a chance to run down his extensive list of triumphs as the world's biggest multimedia superstar. On the kinetic MIB theme song, "Black Suits Comin' (Nod Ya Head)," he rhymes that he's "the best-looking crime fighter since myself in Part 1."

Smith is way past any need to defend his rhymes, and to his credit, he stays true to himself. The worst thing in the world would be for him to sell out at this late date for any dubious street cred. Call him corny if you like, but that Big Willie Style that is the fantasy of many is, in fact, his reality.

—Steve Jones

Singer, Producer, Star

Smith was busy with more than just films. In 2002 he again returned to music. He released his third solo album, *Born to Reign*. The album includes the song he did for *Men in Black II*, "Black Suits Comin'." The song made a brief appearance on Billboard's Hot 100 chart. *Entertainment Weekly* felt that the album wasn't bad. But *Entertainment Weekly* also felt it wasn't that exciting. It sold fewer than three hundred thousand copies, the lowest total of any of Smith's albums. Smith followed up *Born to Reign* with yet another greatest hits album later that year.

Smith was also busy with his new production company, Overbrook Entertainment. One of his projects was a TV show about blended families. Called *All of Us*, the show appeared on the UPN network beginning in 2003. Smith made guest appearances on the show. The appearances marked his first return to TV since *The Fresh Prince of Bel-Air*.

Shop talk: Will and Jada talk on the set of *All of Us* while a crew member works in the background.

Even with all of his other projects, Smith didn't take much time off from his movie career. He was soon back on the set of his next science fiction blockbuster, *I, Robot*. The film is based very loosely on the classic robot stories written by Isaac Asimov. In the film, set in 2035, Smith plays a detective investigating a murder involving a robot. The plot is fun and action filled. But the role also appealed to Smith because it touched on issues of prejudice and slavery.

Smith also found himself in the middle of some controversy. In the movie, he had his first nude scene. But the studio decided that audiences in the United States weren't ready for that. So U.S. viewers got a slightly different version of *I, Robot* than the rest of the world. The change bothered Smith. He joked that the shower scene was the most expensive one in the big-budget movie.

I, Robot shares the title of one of Asimov's famous stories. But the plot doesn't follow anything he'd written. This angered many of Asimov's fans. In fact, they claimed that Asimov would have hated the movie. Despite those complaints, the movie opened to huge audiences. It also got good reviews.

The *New York Post* praised the actors and said the film was smart. It earned more than $52 million in its first week. It was the biggest opening weekend at the box office for any of Smith's movies. The film

I, Robot: Will poses with a Japanese-made robot while promoting *I, Robot* in Tokyo, Japan.

went on to gross $347 million worldwide. *I, Robot* once again proved that mixing science fiction, special effects, and Will Smith was a formula for success.

Smith credits his success with blockbusters to choosing the right projects. "I am a serious summer movie fan, and I know the type of movie that needs to be in July," he said. "I have a sense of what audiences want to see. What I hoped to develop with *I, Robot* was the ability to push it forward."

Smith has made a habit of analyzing which movies and which types of movies do well. As he said in an interview in *USA TODAY*, "I study patterns. Nine out of the top 10 biggest movies of all times have special effects; eight out of 10 have creatures in them; seven out of 10 have a love story. So if you want a hit, you might want to throw those in the mix. I just study patterns and try to stand where lightning strikes." He even applies his analytical skills to relationships—other people's. He and Jada study male-female interaction and give advice to friends and relatives.

Meanwhile, Smith continues to stay in shape for any upcoming action movies. He goes to the gym regularly and lifts weights, as well as runs. He seriously watches what he eats too. He does admit, though, that fitness can be a grind. Yet, he's savvy enough to know that aging action heroes can't go on forever. And he stays involved with his kids as they grow older. In fact, his next role was in response to Jaden wanting dad to be in a movie he could watch.

Trevor Gretzky, son of hockey great Wayne Gretzky, is the junior varsity quarterback at Oaks Christian in Westlake Village, California. He throws passes to Will's son Trey. The varsity quarterback at the school? Nick Montana, son of another sports great, Joe Montana.

Change of Pace

As usual, Smith played the lead in his next movie. But his face was never on camera. That was because it was an animated film called *Shark Tale*, released in 2004. Smith was the voice of the lead character, a fish named Oscar. His loud, energetic voice made him perfect for the part. The movie had an all-star cast that included Angelina Jolie, Robert De Niro, Jack Black, and Renée Zellweger. It was a hit with both adults and children.

Then Smith tried something new for him—a romantic comedy called *Hitch*. Smith's own company, Overbrook Enter-

Just voices: *(from left)* Will, Angelina Jolie, and Jack Black promote *Shark Tale* at the Cannes Film Festival in France. Smith's character appears in the top center of the movie poster behind the actors.

tainment, produced the movie. Smith plays a "love doctor" who helps lonely men get dates. The role gave him a chance to return to comedy. The film reminded fans that he was good for more than just science fiction blockbusters.

February 10, 2005

Love Will find a way

<u>From the Pages of USA TODAY</u>

They lean forward and gaze into each other's eyes. Anticipation builds as their lips gently pucker. Suddenly, Kevin James, TV's *King of Queens*, dives in and lays a dainty peck on the mouth of a shocked Will Smith. Cinema's king of the summer blockbuster recoils in mock disgust as he yells, "What the hell was that?"

The initial reaction of the New Yorkers who witnessed the filming of the smooch lesson gone awry for the courtship caper *Hitch*, opening Friday, wasn't much kinder. "They had no idea what the movie was, no idea what the scene was," recalls Smith, who chuckles while seated in a high-rise eatery with a Central Park view the day after the movie's premiere. "All they see is me out on the corner kissing Kevin James. And this black dude screams out, 'Will, no! Uh-uh. Don't do that. Whatcha doing, Will?' "

Much to the delight of his female admirers, the buff-and-polished action hero is finally starring in a romantic comedy. In *Hitch*, he's a lover, not a fighter. There are no aliens to battle. No androids gone amok. No big guns, bad guys or pug dogs wailing disco classics. Instead, the relationship romp is overrun with hapless males in desperate need of guidance on matters of the heart. That is where Smith's *Hitch* comes in. His job is to coach woeful Romeos so they can impress unattainable Juliets. Meanwhile, Hitch must conquer his own commitment fears when he gets an itch for a sassy gossip columnist. Eva Mendes, who plays the tabloid tattler, says of Smith, "God, he's so sexy. Women are going to respond to him in a different way. You really see his vulnerability."

"It was strange for me, stripping it down to essentially just talking," says Smith, 36, of his genre switch. "No blue screens, nothing. To perform honestly and emotionally with a robot, that's a skill I've developed. But I love the interaction between Eva and me. I'm so at home in that romantic space."

—Susan Wloszczyna

Hitch, released in February 2005, was another success, and it earned good reviews. The *Los Angeles Times* said "Smith is a gifted comic actor, and seeing him in a lighthearted comedy, his first romantic lead, is a pure pleasure." The *Minneapolis Star Tribune* said, "This is the sort of role Smith carries off effortlessly, a decent, level-headed all-American guy who's more sensitive than his [muscles] might suggest."

Despite a busy filming schedule, music wasn't far from Smith's mind. In March 2005, he released his next album, *Lost and Found*. The album features the singles "Party Starter" and "Switch." The songs were Smith's biggest hits since "Will2K." They helped boost album sales to more than six hundred thousand. That was a big improvement over *Born to Reign*. Smith himself said he was pleased with *Lost and Found*. He called "Party Starter" a fun song with an international feel.

The Pursuit of Happyness

Late 2006 saw the release of *The Pursuit of Happyness*. The film is the real-life story of Christopher Gardner, a Wall Street broker who

IN FOCUS

International Businessperson

In 2006 Smith began exploring a new opportunity through Overbrook Entertainment. He looked into making movies in India. Overbrook soon announced that it would work with the media company UTV. The companies plan to produce two films for Indian audiences.

Smith has always had an interest in international business. And India has a large population of movie fans. In partnering with UTV, Smith hopes to find a global audience for Overbrook's films.

Based on a true story: *The Pursuit of Happyness* is based on the life of Christopher Gardner *(right)*, shown here with his son Chris at the premiere of the movie in Los Angeles in 2006.

falls on hard times. Gardner had grown up in an abusive home, where he, his siblings, and his mother had lived in constant fear of his father's rage. He resolved that his life would be different. After a childhood spent in and out of foster homes, Chris joined the U.S. Navy as a young man. He then went to work in the medical field before embarking on an uphill journey to become a stockbroker. Although Gardner's journey included the disintegration of his marriage and enduring homelessness with his young son, he made it to become one of the nation's most successful African American businessmen. He is a self-made millionaire and CEO of his own stockbrokerage firm, Gardner Rich and Co, based in Chicago, Illinois. He has toured the United States to give motivational speeches and to tell his inspirational life story to others. Hollywood and Will Smith were listening.

www.usatoday.com

USA TODAY

Life

SECTION D

December 18, 2006

Happyness is a No. 1 film for Will Smith: From rags to $27 million

From the Pages of
USA TODAY

Will Smith, studio executives like to say, could film himself painting a fence and it would open at No. 1.

So it came as little surprise that *The Pursuit of Happyness* was the top film of the weekend—and Smith's 10th movie to open above $20 million. The rags-to-riches story raked in $27 million, according to estimates from Nielsen EDI. Many analysts expected that the film's themes of poverty and homelessness would relegate *Happyness* to about $17 million and third place at best. But executives at Sony Pictures, which released *Happyness*, say those projections underestimated Smith's clout.

"When you open a movie with Will Smith, you're really not taking much of a chance," says Rory Bruer, distribution chief for Sony. "We knew it wasn't a typical movie, but he's not your typical actor."

Indeed, Smith's 10 debuts of $20 million or more is eclipsed only by Tom Cruise, who has opened 11 movies above that mark. And Smith's films make an average of $114 million, according to the Box Office Mojo website.

"He's got a lot of facets as an actor, but it's more than that," Bruer says. "People genuinely like him. They see him as someone who could be their neighbor or best friend. That translates at the box office beyond the movie itself."

—Scott Bowles

Will recounts how he saw Chris Gardner on *20/20*–a popular television news show–and was immediately intrigued. When camera crews followed Chris into the actual bathroom where he and his son were forced to sleep, Smith was so moved that he decided then and there that he was going to make a film of Gardner's life story.

What other prominent Hollywood star fit the lead role better than Will Smith? The film not only propelled Gardner's story farther into the public sphere but also cemented Will's status as a well-rounded actor. For more than a decade, audiences had known that Will was a charming and funny performer. He was the epitome of likability, but moviegoers had rarely been exposed to his more intense, soul-searching side. *The Pursuit of Happyness* demanded that Will come up with a performance as moving and emotional as the story the film was going to tell. He earned Best Actor nominations at the Oscars and the Golden Globe Awards for his efforts.

The title is not just a cute spelling of the word *happiness*. The film takes its name from the words Thomas Jefferson wrote

Second nomination: Will, Jada, and costar Jaden walk the red carpet at the Oscars in 2007. Will was nominated for Best Actor for *The Pursuit of Happyness.*

in the Declaration of Independence, which reads, "We hold these truths to be self-Evident, that all men are created Equal, that they are Endowed By their Creator with Ceartain [certain] unalienable rights, that among these are Life, Liberty, and the pursuit of Happyness." Jefferson's words

USA TODAY Snapshots®

Black History Month

Honors at the Oscars

Five black actors — Forest Whitaker, Will Smith, Jennifer Hudson, Eddie Murphy and Djimon Hounsou — and songwriter Siedah Garrett have been nominated for Oscars this year. Black winners in major categories:

Category	Count
Original song	5[1]
Supporting actor	4
Leading actor	3
Original score	2
Supporting actress	2
Honorary acting	2
Leading actress	1

1 – Award for 2005 was won by a group; the others were individuals

Source: Black Film Center/Archive at Indiana University

By Sam Ward, USA TODAY, 2007

suggest that all U.S. citizens have the right to follow their dreams. This is essentially what *The Pursuit of Happyness* is all about. Considering that Will Smith has devoted his life to following his dreams, no wonder this story appealed to him so much.

One of the more harrowing parts of Chris Gardner's life was the period of homelessness he endured while supporting his five-year-old son. Fortunately, the on-screen relationship between father and son was hailed by critics and audiences as one of the most touching parts of the film. This was due to Will sharing the screen with his real-life son Jaden. Father and son played father and son. And their warm camaraderie charmed critics and viewers alike.

Despite the easy on-screen chemistry Will had with his son, he felt portraying Gardner was a new and often difficult challenge. The role demanded that Will sidestep making audiences like him. It was a new approach to acting that he had only really undertaken during 2003's *Ali*. To faithfully convey the story, Will said that he connected with Chris Gardner. "We looked in one another's eyes. I said, 'I'm going to learn your story and I'm going to tell your story.' And he said, 'Just tell the truth.'" Will wanted to re-create a truthful version of Chris Gardner, but to do so, he would have to adopt some rather unlikable personality traits. Considering his charm was in part what had launched him to stardom, Will was challenged to put his likable qualities aside. But following Chris Gardner's desire to have his life story told accurately, not flatteringly, Will found the balance between winning an audience over and remaining faithful to the real-life subject matter.

In fact, the two men worked closely throughout the film's development. Gardner was finishing his autobiography while Will was filming. Gardner was often on the set, and Will consulted with him regularly. Gardner recalled being initially uncomfortable because Will was obviously studying him. But after getting to know one another, Gardner came to accept the actor's process and even went as far as giving Will a copy of his manuscript to help him with the role. For his part, Will said he especially identified with Gardner's desire to win and with the fundamentally American nature of his story. Will said, "This country's the only place Chris could exist." Critics and audiences responded well to the film. And Will could stand proudly behind yet another successful project but one that hadn't involved aliens or blue screens.

New Challenges

After the success of *The Pursuit of Happyness*, Will took on a different challenge. *I Am Legend* (2007) was based loosely on the 1954 novel by Richard Matheson. In *Legend*, Smith played Robert Neville, who finds himself the only survivor of a deadly infection that has turned other humans into zombies. He seeks to rid the world of the infected. But they have developed ways to suppress their disease and are working to rebuild society—a society where the uninfected, like Smith, are the stuff of legend and the infected are normal. This time Willow Smith got a chance to work on-screen with her famous dad. She played Neville's daughter in flashbacks.

In *Hancock*, out in 2008, Smith played John Hancock, an alcoholic and reluctant superhero. The people of Los Angeles have tired of his destructive methods and the resulting bills and are calling for his departure. Things begin to change when Hancock saves public relations spokesperson, Ray Embrey. Thrilled to be alive, Ray pledges to change Hancock's public image and does. However, Hancock finds true help through Ray's wife, Mary, a woman with answers to his deepest questions.

Family affair: *(clockwise from top left)* Trey, Will, Jada, Willow, and Jaden attend the Los Angeles premiere of *Hancock* in 2008.

July 7, 2008

Smith's fifth big debut on the Fourth

From the Pages of USA TODAY

Thanks to John Hancock, Mr. Smith goes to the record books. *Hancock*, the story of a disillusioned superhero in need of a PR makeover, took in an estimated $66 million over the weekend and put Will Smith atop the ranks of stars with consecutive blockbusters, according to Nielsen EDI.

The movie, which has collected $107.3 million since its release Tuesday night, makes Smith the first actor in Hollywood history to have eight straight movies eclipse $100 million—many of them over the July Fourth holiday.

Despite mixed reviews, there was little question that *Hancock* would give Smith his 12th No. 1 film. He has propelled *Independence Day, Men in Black, Wild Wild West* and *Bad Boys II* to No. 1 debuts on July Fourth weekends, even with middling critical reactions.

"Audiences don't care what critics say; they're going to turn out for anything he does," says Chad Hartigan, analyst for Exhibitor Relations. Hartigan says that part of Smith's appeal is his ability to mix it up. "His specialty is science fiction and action. But he has had huge hits with drama, like *The Pursuit of Happyness*, romantic comedy, like *Hitch*, and animation. Few actors have that kind of range."

But if the "consecutive" caveat is dropped, there are still a few actors ahead of Smith. Tom Hanks has 15 movies that have grossed more than $100 million. Tom Cruise has 14, followed by Eddie Murphy's 13.

Rory Bruer, distribution chief for Sony Pictures, which released *Hancock*, says the surprising statistic is Smith's overseas allure. *Hancock* opened in 50 other countries this weekend; it was No. 1 in 47 of them, raking in another $78 million. "Certainly, Will Smith has dominated the Fourth of July," Bruer says. "But, frankly, anytime he opens a movie, you're in good shape."

—Scott Bowles

In *Seven Pounds*, which opened in late 2008, Smith played a suicidal IRS agent who is grappling with guilt over past mistakes. He sets out on a journey of redemption by helping seven strangers and, in the meantime, falls in love with one of the people he set out to help.

Fanfare: Will poses with a crowd of fans at the London, England, premiere of *Seven Pounds* in 2009.

Smith has work lined up on several films that should keep him in the box office spotlight well into the next decade. Some he's producing through Overbrook and acting in, with timelines for release yet to be determined. Among these is a project tentatively titled *Empire*. The movie chronicles the life of a contemporary global media mogul. Smith has said he's very excited about another future project, *The Last Pharaoh*. He will play the Nubian pharaoh, Taharqa, around 677 B.C., as he defends ancient Egypt against the Assyrian king Esarhaddon.

IN F🔍CUS

A Big Show

Among his many charitable events, Smith took part in one of the biggest concerts in history. Hundreds of thousands of music fans watched him at the Live 8 show in Philadelphia, while millions more watched on TV. The 2005 show was part of a series of benefit concerts to help poor countries. During the show, Smith asked world leaders to help end the poverty in Africa. He led the audience in snapping their fingers once every three seconds. That's how often a child in Africa dies.

Helping out: Will kicks off the Live 8 concert in Philadelphia, Pennsylvania.

At the same time, Smith and his wife continue their work to give back to their communities, particularly their hometowns of Philadelphia and Baltimore. The Will and Jada Smith Family Foundation funds projects that benefit inner-city kids and their communities. They also support causes that address home violence, AIDS prevention, education, and world poverty.

Will and Jada were also among the many celebrities on hand enjoying the festivities surrounding the inauguration of President Barack Obama. They were present at the swearing-in ceremony and attended balls before and after the ceremony. Will admitted he expected to both cry and cheer during all the events.

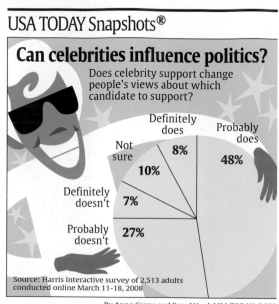

USA TODAY Snapshots®

Can celebrities influence politics?

Does celebrity support change people's views about which candidate to support?

- Definitely does 8%
- Probably does 48%
- Not sure 10%
- Definitely doesn't 7%
- Probably doesn't 27%

Source: Harris Interactive survey of 2,513 adults conducted online March 11-18, 2008

By Anne Carey and Sam Ward, USA TODAY, 2008

Smith has not ruled out playing President Barack Obama, if a project were developed. Both the actor and the president noted the similarities around the ears!

In addition, Will was a standout during the Academy Awards ceremony, where he announced the winner of the most-coveted Best Picture award to *Slum Dog Millionaire*. Afterward, he and many other

History in the making: Will and his family joined more than one million people in Washington, D.C., to watch the inauguration of President Barack Obama in 2009.

top-rated stars partied at the ball hosted by fashion magazine *Vanity Fair*. Meanwhile, a survey conducted by *Forbes* magazine of movie industry professionals named Will as the most bankable film star. With a perfect 10 rating, he beat out Johnny Depp, Leonardo DiCaprio, and Brad Pitt!

Will Smith is one of Hollywood's hardest-working stars. From ordinary beginnings in Philadelphia, Smith has surprised everyone. He took on the worlds of rap, TV, and movies and conquered them all. The Fresh Prince didn't just carve out a small niche in Hollywood. He became one of the biggest movie stars on the planet. With a history like that, it's hard to imagine what he might do next. He once said that he wanted to be the president of the United States. It might have been only a joke. But with Will Smith, almost anything seems possible.

TIMELINE

1965 Jeff "DJ Jazzy Jeff" Townes is born in Philadelphia, Pennsylvania.

1968 Willard C. Smith Jr. is born in West Philadelphia on September 25.

1971 Jada Pinkett is born in Baltimore, Maryland.

1980 Will Smith discovers rap music.

1981 Will's parents divorce.

1982 Will attends Overbrook High. Will forms a rap group called Ready Rock-C with Clarence Holmes. Will calls himself the Fresh Prince.

1985 Will meets DJ Jazzy Jeff.

1986 DJ Jazzy Jeff and the Fresh Prince release "Girls Ain't Nothing but Trouble."

1987 *Rock the House* is released.

1988 *He's the DJ, I'm the Rapper* is released.

1989 DJ Jazzy Jeff and the Fresh Prince win two American Music Awards for Favorite Rap Album and Favorite Rap Artists (*below, pictured with fellow nominee Flavor Flav*). "Parents Just Don't Understand" receives

a Grammy nomination in a new category, Best Rap Performance. *And in This Corner...* is released.

1990   The first episode of *The Fresh Prince of Bel-Air* is broadcast on NBC.

1991   DJ Jazzy Jeff and the Fresh Prince release *Homebase*. Will becomes engaged to Sheree Zampino.

1992   *Homebase* receives a Grammy Award. Will—as well as his show, *The Fresh Prince of Bel-Air*—win Image Awards from the National Association for the Advancement of Colored People. Will and Sheree are married. Willard C. Smith III (Trey) is born.

1993   Will stars in the film adaptation of John Guare's play *Six Degrees of Separation*.

1994   Will stars in the blockbuster action film *Bad Boys*.

1995   Will and Sheree divorce. Will stars in the science fiction hit, *Independence Day*. Will starts dating Jada Pinkett.

1996   The last episode of *The Fresh Prince of Bel-Air* is taped.

1997   Will and Tommy Lee Jones star in the science fiction comedy, *Men In Black*. Will records his first solo album titled *Big Willie Style*. He and Jada get married.

1998   Will stars in *Enemy of the State*. Jaden Smith is born to Will and Jada. Will wins a Grammy for "Men In Black" and performs at the ceremony *(right)*.

1999   *Wild Wild West*, starring Will Smith and Kevin Kline, is released to poor reviews. Will wins another Grammy for "Gettin' Jiggy Wit It." *Willennium* is released.

2000   Will begins work on the Michael Mann film *Ali*. Will travels to Africa for filming. Will and Jada have a daughter named Willow.

2001   *Ali* is released in theaters.

2002   Will is nominated for an Oscar and a Golden Globe for his role in *Ali*. Smith receives the Best Actor award from the BET Awards and Best Performance from the MTV Movie Awards. Will reunites with Tommy Lee Jones for *Men in Black II* and with Martin Lawrence for *Bad Boys II*. Will releases his third solo album *Born to Reign*.

2003   Will stars in *I, Robot*, which is based upon a novel by Isaac Asimov. A TV show, *All of Us*, became one of the first projects produced by Will's new production company, Overbrook Entertainment.

2004   Will lends his voice to the animated feature film, *Shark Tale*.

2005   The romantic comedy *Hitch* is released. Will's album *Lost and Found* comes out.

2006   Will and his son Jaden *(right)* star in *The Pursuit of Happyness*, which earns Will his second Academy Award nomination.

2007 Will stars in *I Am Legend*. Willow has a small part in the movie.

2008 Will stars in *Hancock* and *Seven Pounds*.

2009 Will and Jada attend the historic inauguration of Barack Obama *(below)*.

GLOSSARY

audition: a trial performance. In an audition, an actor tries out for a part by reading a bit of script for the director or producers.

blue screen: a technique for filming special effects scenes. The actors play their parts in front of a big blue screen. Computers later exchange the blue in the picture with special effects.

DJ: short for "disc jockey." DJs are musicians who use record albums and a turntable to create new sounds. DJs often play the background music for rap.

hip-hop: another word for "rap." Hip-hop can also refer to the background music that accompanies rappers.

homophobia: fear of or discrimination against gay people

pilot: the first episode of a new television show

producer: the person who oversees the planning and financing of a television show, movie, record, or other form of entertainment

rap: danceable music with spoken lyrics

screenplay: the script and filming directions for a movie or a television show

sitcom: short for "situation comedy." A sitcom is a humorous television show.

syndication: selling the rights to a show directly to individual TV stations rather than to a network

turntable: a type of record player often used by rap and hip-hop DJs

typecast: to be thought of as capable of playing only a specific kind of role

FILMOGRAPHY

Where the Day Takes You
Role: Manny
Fee: $50,000
Released: 1992
Director: Marc Rocco

Made in America
Role: Tea Cake Walters
Fee: $115,000
Released: 1993
Director: Richard Benjamin

Six Degrees of Separation
Role: Paul
Fee: $500,000
Released: 1993
Director: Fred Schepisi

Bad Boys
Role: Mike Lowrey
Fee: $2.2 million
Released: 1995
Director: Michael Bay

Independence Day
Role: Captain Steven "Eagle" Hiller
Fee: $5 million
Released: 1996
Director: Roland Emmerich

Men in Black
Role: Agent J
Fee: $5 million
Released: 1997
Director: Barry Sonnenfeld

Enemy of the State
Role: Robert Clayton Dean
Fee: $14 million
Released: 1998
Director: Tony Scott

Wild Wild West
Role: James West
Fee: $7 million plus royalties
Released: 1999
Director: Barry Sonnenfeld

The Legend of Bagger Vance
Role: Bagger Vance
Fee: $10 million
Released: 2000
Director: Robert Redford

Ali
Role: Muhammad Ali
Fee: $20 million
Released: 2001
Director: Michael Mann

Men in Black II
Role: Agent J
Fee: $20 million plus royalties
Released: 2002
Director: Barry Sonnenfeld

Bad Boys II
Role: Mike Lowrey
Fee: $20 million plus royalties
Released: 2003
Director: Michael Bay

I, Robot
Role: Del Spooner
Fee: $28 million
Released: 2004
Director: Alex Proyas

Shark Tale
Role: Voice of Oscar
Fee: $15 million
Released: 2004
Directors: Bibo Bergeron, Vicky Jenson, and Rob Letterman

Hitch
Role: Alex "Hitch" Hitchens
Fee: $20 million
Released: 2005
Director: Andy Tennant

The Pursuit of Happyness
Role: Chris Gardner
Fee: $20 million
Released: 2006
Director: Gabriele Muccino

I Am Legend
Role: Robert Neville
Fee: $25 million
Released: 2007
Director: Francis Lawrence

Hancock
Role: John Hancock
Fee: $20 million plus royalties
Released: 2008
Director: Peter Berg

Seven Pounds
Role: Ben Thomas
Fee: $25 million
Released: 2008
Director: Gabriele Muccino

DISCOGRAPHY

Rock the House
Label: Word-Up, Jive/Zomba
Released: 1987

He's The DJ, I'm the Rapper
Label: Jive/Zomba
Released: 1988

And in This Corner . . .
Label: Jive/Zomba
Released: 1989

Homebase
Label: Jive/Zomba
Released: 1991

Code Red
Label: Jive/Zomba
Released: 1993

Big Willie Style
Label: Columbia
Released: 1997

Greatest Hits
Label: Jive
Released: 1998

Willennium
Label: Columbia
Released: 1999

Before the Willennium
(greatest hits)
Label: BMG
Released: 2000

Born to Reign
Label: Columbia
Released: 2002

Will Smith—
Greatest Hits
Label: Columbia
Released: 2002

Lost and Found
Label: Interscope
Released: 2005

The Very Best of D. J.
Jazzy Jeff &
the Fresh Prince
Label: Jive/Zomba
Released: 2006

SOURCE NOTES

8　Brian J. Robb, *Will Smith: King of Cool* (London: Plexus Publishing, 2000), 13.

8　Ibid., 10.

8　K. S. Rodriguez, *Will Smith: From Fresh Prince to King of Cool* (New York: HarperCollins, 1998), 12.

11　Chris Nickson, *Will Smith* (New York: St. Martin's Press, 1999), 13.

12–13　Robb, 14.

14　Marilyn D. Anderson, *Will Smith* (San Diego: Lucent Books, 2003), 17.

15–16　Nickson, 24.

18　Robb, 27.

20　Ibid., 28.

23　Anne Janette Johnson, "DJ Jazzy Jeff & the Fresh Prince Biography: Contemporary Musicians," *Will Smith and Jazzy Jeff Fan Site*, June 1991, http://www.jazzyjefffreshprince.com/biography/jjfpcontempmusicians.htm (October 18, 2006).

25　Rodriguez, 24.

25　Robb, 34.

26　Ibid., 36.

29　Ibid., 43.

31　Nickson, 48.

31　Tony Fontana, "Biography for Will Smith," *Internet Movie Database*, n.d., http://university.imdb.com/name/nm0000226/bio (October 18, 2006).

34　Nickson, 58.

36　Maggie Marron, *Will Smith: From Rap Star to Mega Star* (New York: Warner Books, 2000), 55.

37　Robb, 63.

39　Anderson, 47.

40　Rodriguez, 57.

43　Nickson, 98.

44　Robb, 76.

45　Ibid., 84.

46　Ibid., 85.

48　Ibid., 89.

51　Nickson, 116.

51 Marron, 75.

52 Rodriguez, 63.

53 Ibid., 82.

53 Robb, 101.

58 Ibid., 111.

59 Ibid., 115.

59 Marron, 65.

69 Cinema, "Will Smith's Insecurity Solved by Muhammad Ali," *Cinema.com*, n.d., http://www.cinema.com/news/item/2842/will-smiths-insecurity-solved-by-muhammad-ali.phtml (October 18, 2006).

71 Anderson, 73.

74 "The Homecoming: 'Ali' Films in Africa," *Regalfilmcentre.com*, n.d., http://www.regalfilmcentre.com/films/ali/more_info/4.html (October 18, 2006).

77 Overbrook, "Back in the Day," *Willsmith.com*, n.d., http://www.willsmith.com/bitd/ (October 18, 2006).

83 Associated Press, "Will Smith Tries New Role in 'I, Robot,'" *CBS46.com*, July 16, 2004, http://www.cbs46.com/ Global/story.asp?S=2048665 (October 18, 2006).

83 Scott Bowles, "Will Smith Has Found the Magic Formula," USA Today.com, June 26, 2008, http://www.usatoday.com/life/movies/news/2008-06-26-will-smith_N.htm (March 31, 2009).

86 Carina Chocano, "Hitch" *Calendarlive.com*, February 11, 2005, http://www.calendarlive.com/movies/chocano/cl-et-hitch11feb11,1,5175101.story (October 18, 2006).

86 Colin Covert, *Minneapolis Star Tribune*, 2005, quoted in "Hitch (2005)," *Rotten Tomatoes*, n.d., http://www.rottentomatoes.com/m/hitch/ (October 18, 2006).

90 Lemuel Haynes, "Lemuel Haynes, a New England Mulatto, Attacks Slavery, 1776" in Richard D. Brown, ed., *Major Problems in the Era of the American Revolution, 1760–1791* (Boston, Houghton Mifflin Company, 2000).

90–91 Rebecca Murray, "Will Smith Talks about 'The Pursuit of Happyness,'" *About.com*, n.d., http://movies.about.com/od/thepursuitofhappyness/a/pursuitws120806.htm (March 31, 2009).

91 Ibid.

SELECTED BIBLIOGRAPHY

Anderson, Marilyn D. *Will Smith*. San Diego: Lucent Books, 2003.

Berenson, Jan. *Will Power!* New York: Simon & Schuster, 1997.

Marron, Maggie. *Will Smith: From Rap Star to Mega Star*. New York: Warner Books, 2000.

Nickson, Chris. *Will Smith*. New York: St. Martin's Press, 1999.

Robb, Brian J. *Will Smith: King of Cool*. London: Plexus Publishing, 2000.

Rodriguez, K. S. *Will Smith: From Fresh Prince to King of Cool*. New York: HarperCollins, 1998.

Stern, Dave. *Will Smith*. New York: Simon & Schuster, 1997.

FURTHER READING AND WEBSITES

Ayazi-Hashjin, Sherry. *Rap and Hip Hop: The Voice of a Generation*. New York: Rosen, 1999.

Baker, Soren. *The History of Rap and Hip Hop*. San Diego: Lucent Books, 2006.

Corrigan, Jim. *Will Smith*. Broomall, PA: Mason Crest, 2007.

Friedman, Lise. *Break a Leg! The Kids' Guide to Acting & Stagecraft*. New York: Workman Publishing, 2002.

Greene, Meg. *Will Smith*. Philadelphia: Chelsea House Publishers, 2002.

The Internet Movie Database
http://www.imdb.com
This online resource allows you to look up movies, actors, plot summaries, and more. The site includes a biography of Will Smith as well as a list of his projects.

McCracken, Kristin. *Will Smith*. New York: Children's Press, 2000.

Powers, Tom. *Steven Spielberg*. Minneapolis: Lerner Publications Company, 2005.

Reeves, Diane Lindsey. *Career Ideas for Kids Who Like Music and Dance*. New York: Facts on File, 2001.

Schulman, Arlene. *Muhammad Ali*. Minneapolis: Lerner Publications Company, 2005.

Schuman, Michael A. *Will Smith: I Like Blending a Message with Comedy*. Berkeley Heights, NJ: Enslow, 2006.

Stewart, Mark. *Will Smith*. Chicago: Raintree, 2005.

Wiese, Jim. *Movie Science: 40 Mind-Expanding, Reality-Bending, Starstruck Activities for Kids*. New York: John Wiley & Sons, 2001.

Will Smith: Official Website
http://www.willsmith.com
On Smith's official website, you'll find information on his music, movies, and television shows. You can also read an online biography of Smith.

Will Smith Zone
http://www.willsmithzone.com
This fan site includes news on Smith's career, achievements, and latest film and music projects.

INDEX

PHOTO ACKNOWLEDGMENTS

The images in this book are used with the permission of: © Robert Deutsch/ USA TODAY, pp. 1, 67 (right), 100; © George Pimentel/WireImage/Getty Images, p. 3; © Neal Preston/CORBIS, pp. 4, 25; AP Photo/Julie Markes, p. 5; © Dan MacMedan/USA TODAY, pp. 6, 24, 29, 38, 43, 49, 60, 63, 70, 75, 77, 80, 85, 88, 93; © Lambert/Hulton Archive/Getty Images, p. 7; © Dmitriy Karelin/Dreamstime.com, p. 9; © Michael Ochs Archives/Getty Images, p. 10; Classmates Media, Inc., pp. 12, 18; © Raymond Boyd/Michael Ochs Archives/ Getty Images, p. 14; Everett Collection, pp. 16; 22; 46; 54, 84; © David Drapkin/Image Direct/Getty Images, p. 19; © Al Pereira/Michael Ochs Archives/Getty Images, p. 21; AP Photo, p. 23; © Jim Smeal/WireImage/Getty Images, p. 28; Chris Haston/NBCU Photo Bank via AP Images, p. 30; © Bob Riha, Jr./USA TODAY, pp. 32, 62, 81, 89; © Columbia TriStar/Photofest, p. 33; © Miranda Shen/Fotos International/Getty Images, p. 35; © MGM/ZUMA Press, p. 37; © Columbia/courtesy Everett Collection, p. 42; © Milan Ryba/ DMI/Time Life Pictures/Getty Images, p. 45; Vesa Moilanen/Rex Features USA, p. 47; © Daniel Haller/Dreamstime.com, p. 48; © Charles W. Bush/ Time Life Pictures/Getty Images, p. 50; © Steve Granitz/WireImage/Getty Images, pp. 51, 61; © Eileen Blass/USA TODAY, pp. 55, 68, 99; AP Photo/John Dolan, Ho, p. 57; © Jym Wilson/USA TODAY, p. 58; © ALLIED FILM MAKERS/ ZUMA Press, p. 64; © M. Caulfield/WireImage/Getty Images, p. 66; © Robert Hanashiro/USA TODAY, pp. 67 (left), 105; © LUCY NICHOLSON/AFP/Getty Images, p. 69; © Agence France Presse/Getty Images, p. 73; © Columbia Pictures/ZUMA Press, p. 74; © Vince Bucci/Getty Images, p. 76; © Elie S. Azoulay/Visual/ZUMA Press, p. 78; © Peter Freed/USA TODAY, p. 79; © Koichi Kamoshida/Getty Images, p. 82; © Charley Gallay/Getty Images, p. 87; Patrick Rideaux/Rex Features USA, p. 92; © Eamonn McCormack/WireImage/Getty Images, p. 94; © William Thomas Cain/Getty Images, p. 95; © Evan Eile/ USA TODAY, p. 97; © DMI/Time Life Pictures/Getty Images, p. 98; © H. Darr Beiser/USA TODAY, p. 101; © Todd Plitt/USA TODAY, p. 104.

Front cover: © Mike Marsland/WireImage/Getty Images.
Back cover: © Dan MacMedan/USA TODAY.

ABOUT THE AUTHOR

Matt Doeden is a freelance author and editor living in Minnesota. He's written and edited hundreds of children's books on topics ranging from genetic engineering to rock climbing to monster trucks.